Use Me, Lord

Incredible Miracles happen for those who believe

Helena Ohmen

God can "use you" in
Amazing ways!!"
You only need to be
Obedient and Bold!

May this book encourage
you to be Both!

Helen

Dedication

✝

I dedicate this book to my precious

granddaughter

'Aleisha Christina Marie'

Who puts the joy in my daily step

And adds her sweet fragrance to my life.

The angels danced the day

She was born.

Chapters

Foreword

If anyone would come after me, he must deny himself and take up his cross and follow me, for whosoever wants to save his life will lose it, but whosoever loses his life for me and for the gospel will save it. What good is it for a man to gain the whole world, yet forfeit his soul? Or what can a man give in exchange for his soul? If anyone is ashamed of me and my words in this adulterous and sinful generation, the Son of man will be shamed of him when he comes in his Father's glory with the holy angels. Mark 8: 34-38

The most important one is this: Hear, O Israel, the Lord our God, the Lord is one. Love the Lord your God with all your heart and with all your soul and with all your mind and with all your strength. The second is this: Love your neighbor as yourself, there is no commandment greater than these. Mark 12: 29-31

Watch out that no one deceives you. Many will come in my name, claiming, 'I am He,' and will deceive many. When you hear of wars and rumors of wars, do not be alarmed. Such things must happen, but the end is still to come. Nation will rise against nation, and Kingdom against Kingdom. There will be earthquakes in various places, and famines. These are the beginning of birth pains. Mark 13: 5-8 Brother will betray brother to death and a father his child. Children will rebel against their parents and have them put to death. All men will hate you because of me, but he who stands firm to the end will be saved. Mark 13: 12-13

Go into all the world and preach the good news to all creation. Whoever believes and is baptized will be saved, but whoever does not believe will be condemned. And these signs will accompany those who believe: In my name they will drive out demons; they will speak in new tongues; ... they will place their hands on sick people, and they will get well. Mark 16: 15-18

For God so loved the world that He gave his one and only Son, that whoever believes in him shall not perish but have eternal life. John 3: 16

Unless you people see miraculous signs and wonders, you will never believe. John 4: 48 "Go to this people and say, You will be ever hearing but never understanding; you will be ever seeing but never perceiving. For this people's heart has become calloused; they hardly hear with their ears, and they have closed their eyes, otherwise they might see with their eyes, hear with their ears, understand with their hearts and turn, and I would heal them." Acts 28: 26-27

Do not stop him, No one who does a miracle in my name can in the next moment say anything bad about me, for whosoever is not against us is for us. I tell you the truth; anyone who gives you a cup of water in my name because you belong to Christ will certainly not lose his reward. Mark 9:39-41

I am the light of the world. Whoever follows me will never walk in darkness, but will have the light of life. John 8: 12

My sheep listen to my voice; I know them, and they follow me. I give them eternal life, and they shall never perish; no one can snatch them out of my hand. My Father, who has given them to me, is greater than all; no one can snatch them out of my Father's hand. I and the Father are one. John: 27- 30

I am the way and the truth and the life. No one comes to the Father except through me. If you really knew me, you would know my Father as well. From now on, you do know him and have seen him. John 14: 6-7

"In the last days," God says, "I will pour out my spirit on all people. Your sons and your daughters will prophesy, your young men will see visions, your old men will dream dreams, Even on my servants, both men and women, I will pour out my Spirit in those days, and they will prophesy. I will show wonders in the heaven above and signs on the earth below, blood and fire and billows of smoke, the sun will be turned to darkness and the moon to blood before the coming of the great and glorious day of the Lord. And everyone who calls on the Lord will be saved." Acts 2: 17-21

Behold, I am coming soon! My reward is with me, and I will give to everyone according to what he has done. I am the Alpha and the Omega, the first and the last, the beginning and the end. Blessed are those who wash their robes, that they may have the right to the tree of life and may go through the gates into the city. Outside are the dogs, those who practice magic arts, the sexually immoral, the murderers, the idolaters and everyone who loves and practices falsehood. I, Jesus, have sent my angel to give you this testimony for the churches. I am the root and the offspring of David, and the bright Morning Star. Revelations 22: 12-17

Yes, I am coming soon. Revelations 22: 20

Jesus Christ

Introduction

✝

The Lord has been on my heart to write this book for over two years. I used every excuse for my procrastination including how busy I was with my job. I worked long hours and as anyone in my family will attest, I am a workaholic. God has been patient and has graciously listened to my excuses, as I continued my career and delayed my assignment. I have come to realize, sometimes through trials, that when God says "Do it," He is serious about the assignment. So, when I lost what I thought was my dream job, God allowed me a few days of self pity and crying before saying, "Now write the book." So, here I am, writing my first book. After writing the first eight chapters, I was laying in bed one night thinking about the Foreword for the book. I always thought the foreword was extremely important to be written by someone who was already well known, as it would draw people to read something by an unknown author, since they were already familiar with the author of the Foreword. As I lay there awake, I was thinking that some of the best Christian books I had read were written by people like Tommy Tenny, John Hagee, Joyce Myers, or Benny Hinn. How awesome it would be to get one of them to write the foreword for this book, yet I surely had no contacts that could assist me with that huge order. While laying there in bed, talking to the Lord, He made it very clear that the foreword would be written by "Jesus Christ." Now, understand, that when I talk with God, it's like you and I holding a conversation.

There are no "thee and thou" or long drawn out empty prayers. When that still small voice of the Holy Spirit said, "Jesus Christ," would write the foreword, I immediately said, "God, they will think I'm crazy!" "It would be ridiculous and preposterous for me to even consider writing a foreword and signing the name of Jesus Christ to it." The small voice of the Holy Spirit became much louder and bolder now, and I knew that I was being reprimanded by my Heavenly Father, "You already have His words in my book. You will use the words He has said, which are already written. I will show you. There are people who will read this book, who have never read the Bible enough themselves to know my truth." OK Lord... Use me Lord! Sometimes you need to tell me two or three times, yet I will come around eventually.

Now that we have that explanation about the Foreword out of the way, I would like to give a back ground of how I got to the point of writing this book. Unlike most Christian authors, I am not a Pastor, have no formal theology training, and for all intensive purposes, just an ordinary everyday person. I believe that the relevance of this book is so important and ordained by God, that you hear from someone who is not formally trained in theology and not a professional working in the ministry. The impact of allowing God to 'use me,' would then become a close-up series of events, to which you can personally relate. It's like those 'dummy books' that have circulated on most all subjects, which makes it so easy for readers to understand various topics. Although, I don't believe that I've seen one written as *Christianity for Dummies*, this book is meant to be read in that simple to understand format. The chapters of this book are a small sampling of events where God has used me to touch the lives of others, while allowing me to grow closer to my spiritual destiny. As each event occurred, I too was in amazement that God was so powerful and allowed me the privilege to be his hands and voice. I am always careful to direct all the praise, glory and honor to God, as I am merely the vessel, while God is the power and source.

I was raised in New Jersey to a non-practicing Christian family. For some reason unknown to me, my Mother would drop my brother and me off at Sunday school every week and then return to retrieve us. As I ponder on that now, it amazes me that we went to Sunday school at all. Those early days of attending Sunday school formed the foundation of my beliefs. My parents would make the customary visits to church on Easter and Christmas with the façade of living the Christian life. It was not until my parents were in their 50's that they received Jesus as their personal savior and then were indeed true Christians. I have very limited memory prior to the age of 6 years old and was raised in fear to obey my parents. My father was from a large family of 12 children and had been raised on a farm, having worked on the farm at a very early age. He was not a loving and tender father and hugs were far and few between. Any attempt by my father to provide a hug would feel robotic and stiff, as there was no tenderness in his arms. My Mother was more of a hugger for 'show' when people were around and the tenderness I had longed for was not obtained there either. Condemnation was a common verbal event in the house, and as children, we soon learned to keep peace and be obedient, if we didn't want the *belt*. My parents both had unresolved baggage from their childhood which prevented them from being gentle and loving parents. I had committed at an early age to be a loving, caring, affectionate, supportive Mother and had asked God to make me a loving and Godly Mother. I knew from my first memories that I wanted to be a nurse. Upon graduation from high school I entered Nursing School to become a Registered Nurse. While I was in nursing school, I dated Fred. I graduated from Nursing School and married my husband Fred the same year, in 1979. Fred is eleven years older than me, and had been married before with one child. As I write this book, Fred and I have been married for 31 years. Fred and I have two children together, David and Jessica, who are now married and living nearby. I have one precious granddaughter Aleisha and hopes of more. My husband Fred and I had attended a *word of Life* event that had come to the area and we both received Jesus as our Personal Savior on October 24, 1984. I was 27 years old at the time and was excited about God's plans for my life. I can remember hearing for the first time that the prayer of salvation is the *first prayer* God hears from you. I had never heard that before, and frankly, I could not understand it. During my childhood, I had many answered prayers. I also recall, all my life, knowing that if God would *show* me something bad that was going to happen, I would speak words to stop it from happening. That was a powerful tool, which only recently did I come to realize was a *special gift* from God. Growing up, it was just normal for me to know when bad things were about to happen and that I could just ask God to prevent them. As I reflected on that whole *first prayer* concept, I asked God, If that was true, had I indeed asked him to be my personal savior at an early age, that I could not remember? God was quick to give me a full-colored vision of myself at the age of about 5 years old. I was sitting on my bed room floor in an aqua colored checked dress. My hair was parted on one side and pulled across to the other side and held with a small plastic barrette. It appeared that I had just returned from Sunday school, as I had on white socks with lace on the edges and black patented leather shoes. I was sitting with a small Bible in my hands and was saying "Jesus, come into my heart." I must have heard about salvation in Sunday school that day and as a child understood what I needed to say. It had been a simple prayer of a 5 year old child, but really all that needed to be said. I am so thankful that people had committed themselves to teaching Sunday school and I am grateful for that special someone who was most-likely unaware of the impact they had made on a small girl that day.

As you read the chapters in this book, I ask that you read slowly and digest the experience. We live in a fast and speed-reading world.

Allow your spirit to capture the contents and ask God, what this can personally mean for you. Have you allowed God to *use you* or, have you ignored that small voice? I remember someone saying one time, that to hear the voice of God was like singing *Happy Birthday* in your mind. That really is what it's like. You are hearing words in your mind. The words you are hearing are not your own thoughts. The words of God are always encouraging and good. God would never tell you to do something evil or to hurt someone. If you have bad or evil thoughts in your mind, it is not God and you must tell them to *go away in the name of Jesus.*

Over the years I have regularly written in my journals. Through this documentation of events and times that God has used me to his glory, I was able to recall details to include in this book. I would encourage you to write in a journal, so you can later review and reflect on your spiritual progress. My journals are full of miracles and times that God has used me to his glory. This book is a mere sampling of experiences where God has allowed me to be used for His purposes. It is without boasting or pride that I share these precious events. I am careful to make this less about me and all about him. This is all about Jesus. To God be all the Glory! The Holy Spirit has revealed to me that this book will be anointed with emotions. You will laugh and cry throughout the book which will reflect the same places that I laughed and cried as it was written. May you be blessed reading these events knowing that if *I can do this*, you can also do these things, in the name of Jesus and through the power of your Heavenly Father. The only requirement is that you must have received Jesus Christ as your personal savior. Salvation is the greatest Miracle of All!

May you be blessed as you read this book and may Our Heavenly Father open your eyes to the plans He has for your life. May you hear the voice of the Holy Spirit clearly and be brave enough to respond to his assignments regardless of what you feel others may think. Stepping forward will bless you beyond your imagination and may very well be the answer to someone's prayer. A few years ago the Holy Spirit prompted me to discuss my faith with the President and CEO of the company that I was working for and to pray with him for increased discernment. I trembled at the thought of this assignment yet knew God's plans are always perfect and right on time. The morning I met with the president and CEO of that company and told him that the Holy Spirit had told me to meet with him, discuss my faith, and to pray with him for discernment. He was delighted and grabbed my hands immediately to pray. He had asked the Lord for discernment and his prayer was answered that day. Later, he told me that his eyes had been opened during a meeting that very afternoon and he was able to see into the hearts and actual intent of his management leaders. Stepping forward that day developed a friendship with that sweet man that will last a lifetime. I no longer work for that company, yet we remain spirit-to-spirit connected and I am often prompted to pray for his success. Fulfilling that assignment not only changed his life, it changed the lives of everyone that works in that company. You can never know the impact that the completion of your assignment will bring. Be brave and tell your Lord... "Use me Lord!"

In Christ's precious love,

Helena

Chapter 1

When God says Move

✝

I had always attended the same Baptist church in a small northern New Jersey town. That small Baptist Church in northern New Jersey was the church I had attended as a child and the same church in which I was married in June of 1979. I knew everyone who attended and knew it was *my* church. My husband Fred and I had our *regular* pew where we sat with our two children each Sunday. It was the church where our two children David and Jessica were dedicated to the Lord as babies, and the same church in which I had been baptized years earlier. That church was all I ever knew. I knew that there were other denominations and had often heard about those *holy rollers* and *fanatics.* I had never allowed myself to even consider visiting those types of places. No one in my family was considered overly religious. We attended church, threw a few dollars in the offering plate when it passed by, and volunteered time when pressed to assist with areas such as Sunday school, the nursery or vacation Bible school. I was a Baptist, had accepted Jesus Christ as my savior, and I was all set. Or, so I thought!

My father's mother, my Grandmother; Delci, was the most religious person I had known as a child. We didn't visit her often because she was frequently in and out of mental hospitals and apparently not a stable environment to visit with children. She passed away when I was about 9 years old. I remember her talking about

Jesus and feeling the love she had for her Lord and Savior. I remember as a child, that when I sat on her lap, I always felt like I was vibrating. Looking back I realize that she must have had *the gift.* It is truly a gift, to be filled with the Holy Spirit. Being so young, I was unaware of what may have happened in her life that lead her to be put into mental hospitals, and only now am I starting to see why that may have been. When people have the Holy Spirit working in their lives and are acting in the gifts of the spirit, people often think they are crazy. She was probably hearing the voice of God and telling others. I only wish I could have been older, so I could have known her better. I will see her when I get to Heaven because I know she will be waiting there for me, but more about that in another chapter.

Grandma's funeral was unlike any I have ever attended. She had told everyone that she wanted all of her family and friends to wear white clothes to her funeral. She wanted everyone to know that this was not to be a mourning of her death, but a celebration of her life and having full knowledge that she was with her Heavenly Father in heaven. So, we all wore white. I had to have a new outfit for the funeral, since I had nothing in white that was dressy enough to wear to a funeral. My parents bought me a 2-piece white crinkle material skirt and blazer. Crinkle material was really in style back then, so I was overjoyed to have something in-style to wear to the funeral. Unfortunately after the funeral, my mother decided to dye the white blazer and white skirt to a shade of navy blue, without first washing it. The areas of perspiration under the arms of the blazer, took the navy blue dye much darker, so I was never able to wear that lovely blazer again. What a waste of a great outfit. What a glorious event that funeral was. With all that white in one room it looked like the place was full of angels. Of course Grandma also was wearing a white dress in her casket. I know that it's not possible, but I swear, Grandma looked like she was smiling at me when I went to the casket to see her. I never told anyone that until now, because, you know... you would think I was crazy. As a child of 9 years old, that left a huge impact on me, one that makes me smile to this day.

When the Holy Spirit starts changing your heart, it starts with small desires and increases in intensity. That was me! I was feeling restless in my spirit, yet I could not even explain to my husband what it was all about. I went through the routine week after week, attending the same Baptist church, leaving each Sunday, feeling like I was missing something. Now, mind you, I have nothing bad to say about being a Baptist.

I am proud that I was raised a Baptist, because it gave me strong roots and sound doctrine.

I knew something 'big' was about to happen. I started feeling restlessness and felt like we were supposed to move. Move? Not just move from that church to another church, but move from New Jersey to another state. Wow, that was huge in itself for me, as I had lived in the same town all my life and actually in the same house until I was married. The same house my parents had lived in since they were married back in 1950. My parent's house was built and enlarged over several years, piece-by-piece as they could afford to expand it. It started as a 2 room cottage with an outhouse. Adding on and building up for a second story, the house eventually had 3 bedrooms, one bathroom inside and a two car garage. The closest house was my grand-parents home. It was special to live next to my mother's parents, as I always had a place to go when I felt in need of an extra hug. I called them Nana and Papa. Papa had often talked about living through the great depression and never feeling it, since they lived totally off the land. They grew their own garden and Nana canned the harvest, which they ate all year. I remember Nana and Papa raising chickens, pigs, and a cow. When Fred and I married, we just moved across town. The same town I had lived the first 22 years of my life. Our family was proud of the stability and roots, which many families did not have in those times.

How do you discuss with your husband and two children that you feel we are supposed to move? All our family members were there. All our friends were there. No one from my family had ever moved away before. As I struggled to approach the subject with my husband, the words would never come. This went on for weeks and weeks and I felt like I was carrying a huge burden. I finally prayed "Lord, you tell him... if this is something we are supposed to do... you tell him." That would be the first of many times I would pray that simple prayer.

To my amazement, that prayer was answered! Within a few days, my husband asked me if I had ever thought about moving. Moving? Did he ask me if I ever thought about moving? Wow! Well that started a discussion about where would be a nice place to move to. That day was also the first time, the first verifiable time, that I knew God spoke to my husband. Although, he didn't realize it yet, he thought that it was just his own brilliant idea. Isn't that just like a man?

Living in New Jersey, the winters were cold and long. The thought of not having to deal with snow was a welcome thought. Fred and I discussed which states still had snow and cool weather, yet not as significant as we had in New Jersey. I loved the change of seasons and seeing the trees change colors in the fall, so I really wanted to move someplace where that was still possible.

That year, when we took a family vacation to Florida, we decided to drive from New Jersey to Florida. I believe the year was 1989 and in those days there were no navigation systems to get you where you were going. It was the old truth-worthy map. You know the map, the one which comes so nicely folded and never looks like that again. I knew there was a trick to getting it folded back up, but since I usually folded the map to visualize the current location, the map had so many folds, in the end there was no way to know where the original folds had been in the first place.

As we were traveling down to Florida through Tennessee on I-81, I remember saying to my husband Fred that the beauty of the area took my breath away. The sun was shining and the greens were so clean and bright. I don't remember ever seeing such vibrant green leaves and green grass, and the mountains! The mountains were awesome to look at. I had never seen mountains look so beautiful before. The mountains looked like velvet rippling and folding from the peaks to the base. I realize now, looking back and reflecting on this time in my life, that God was drawing us to this area and putting such a love in our hearts for the area. It was not just a love for the landscape, but a love for the people who lived there. Fred broke my thoughts by saying, "circle this spot on the map, so we can check it out when we get home." I did just that. I made a 3 inch circle with an ink-pen around the place we were traveling through at that very moment.

When we returned home from our Florida vacation, I checked out the area I had circled on the map. It was a small town called White Pine, Tennessee. It was a very small town, yet had an elementary school with a great reputation. I called the school and spoke with the principal. He sounded kind and well educated. To my amazement, he mentioned that a group of mothers met at the school each morning in the upper loft, to pray for the school and the students. Unbelievable! In New Jersey, they were taking prayer out of the school and here they had mothers praying *in* the school. I was concerned, since my son had a learning disability, that a small school would not have the resources to provide for his educational needs. The principal assured me that they did indeed have classes for my son in the school and some of the best special education teachers in the state. The principal proudly shared the school's test scores, which were among the highest in the state. That was very important to me, since I did not want my children's education to be substandard. I had always heard that the south was slow, so I feared the education would be lacking. In actuality, when we moved to Tennessee, my children had to 'catch-up' since the White Pine Elementary school was ahead of the school they had previously attended in New Jersey. Now, who would have thought that? I checked out the towns in the surrounding area and soon realized there were several hospitals within a short driving distance, so I would have no problem finding work as a Registered Nurse. I knew that the plan... God's plan... was coming together. We contacted a realtor in the next largest town, which was Morristown, Tennessee and discussed what was available.

It is only looking back now that I am able to realize God's plan that I leave *My Nazareth*. The authority that I was going to be given in the name of Jesus and under the power of the Holy Spirit would have little effect in my home town.

Genesis 12:1 The Lord said to Abram, "Leave your country, your people and your father's household and go to the land I will show you."

Matthew 13: 57 But Jesus said to them, "Only in his home town and in his own house is a prophet without honor."

Chapter 2

You can't get there from here.

†

We contacted a lovely lady named Margaret from a real estate brokerage in Morristown, Tennessee. She said there were many great homes we would love and several had acreage, which we really wanted for the children.

This was to be a *quick-trip* over a long weekend and we decided to leave the children at home with our parents. We wanted to see as much as possible in a short time and the children were 7 and 9 years old at the time.

We could not imagine that would be much fun for them, nor for us, for that matter. And so, we were off to Tennessee to look for property or a home.

Margaret had given us directions including which exit to get off I-81 and head toward Morristown, Tennessee to meet her at the office. It sounded simple enough. I had always considered myself to be well educated and directions had always come very easily for me. We stayed at the Ramada Inn just off the exit, so we could plan to drive into Morristown the next morning and meet with Margaret. I had it all planned out. I have always been very detail oriented and planning was an area of one of my greatest strengths. We ate breakfast that next morning and headed toward Morristown. I remember feeling so excited, as we were about to start a new chapter in our lives and had no idea what to expect. I was driving and exited the road at the exit marked for Morristown. The area was under construction, so the road veered around and finally headed me onto another highway. We had driven only a short distance, when it dawned on me... we were headed back in the same direction we had just come from. We were indeed on the same highway headed back to the Ramada Inn.

We turned around and headed back toward that Morristown exit again. As I exited the highway on that Morristown exit, I was careful to follow the signs through the construction zone and headed toward Morristown. Fred and I were concentrating very hard to make sure we didn't miss anything this time. We navigated through the construction area and it lead us to a highway. As we entered that highway, we realized once again, that we were back on that same highway headed back to the Ramada Inn.

I said to Fred, "I am so glad the kids are not with us. We are acting totally stupid today." We both laughed and agreed it was time for Fred to drive. If Fred were driving, then I could better look around and help navigate through that construction area and get on the right road. We were both convinced we had missed a road hidden in the construction area.

So, back we went. Fred was driving this time and we exited the highway onto the exit labeled for Morristown, Tennessee. With me not driving, I was able to look around and we realized the detour went through a parking lot of a closed gas station and then wiggled through areas of dirt and gravel road before once again returning us to asphalt. We had it this time! Success! We were not defeated and we felt an accomplishment as we entered the highway labeled Morristown.

Not again! We were once again on that same highway headed back to the Ramada Inn. Feeling total defeated and exhausted, we drove back to the Ramada Inn and called Margaret at the real estate agency. I told her that we had tried several times and could just "not get there from here." I had expected that she would say something smart about our inability to follow directions, but Margaret was so sweet when she said, "I will come and pick you up there. If God is not allowing you to come to Morristown, then you are not supposed to look in Morristown. We will look in White Pine, since that is clearly where God has plans for you." Those words have come back to my memory frequently over the years. Margaret being a more mature Christian realized the value of God directing our every path. I was still in that learning process and was still amazed every time it happened.

We found the most beautiful piece of property with 23 acres. Within the year, we were moving there. We had packed everything we had and left the only place we had ever lived. We moved away from all our family and friends. The reality of the move was over-whelming at times. My daughter Jessica, who was 8 years old at the time, cried when we left, knowing she was leaving her friends behind. All the *what-if's* were always popping up in my mind. I kept reminding myself that this is obviously where God wanted us to be, for some reason.

We looked like the *Beverly Hillbillies* when we made the move from New Jersey to Tennessee. We had rented a 24 foot U-Haul truck, which Fred drove with my son David as his passenger. Jessica and I drove behind in the car. We had two pets to take along, which obviously had to be with us inside the vehicles. We had a parakeet named Sparky in a birdcage strapped in the seat-belt in the back seat of our car. My daughter also had a pet chicken, named Feathers. Yes! Jessica had a pet chicken. Feathers was a member of the family and although not allowed in the house, she followed us everywhere when we were outside. Feathers would rub up against your leg much the same as a cat would do. Feathers was very affectionate for a chicken. Feathers was traveling in a wire cage on the floorboard of the passenger side of the U-Haul truck Fred was driving.

We were driving for several hours when Jessica and I started noticing that when cars passed the U-Haul ahead of us, they would slow up and we would see the people point and laugh. Back in those days we didn't have cell phones, so we couldn't just call them and ask what was so funny up there. After a few miles of watching the apparent entertainment which was happening in the U-Haul truck, which all passing car passengers were enjoying, we decided to pass and see for ourselves. As we got up even with the truck we looked to the right and Fred was looking at us. To our amazement, Feathers was sitting on Fred's right shoulder. As Fred looked to the left, the chicken would also look to her left, but having to lean forward to look around Fred's head. It was the funniest thing I have ever seen in my life. Feathers brought us many hours of entertainment on the trip, which I'm sure was also planned by God to ease the tension of the move. Isn't it just like God to use animals to soften our journey?

Moving things into the house was a huge task, as it had rained that entire weekend and we had no grass planted yet. Our yard was total mud. Not just any mud, but the red mud that stains everything and feels like ice under your feet. The yard was on a slight incline and we could not even get the U-Haul truck close to the house. The truck was about 100 feet away from the house, where it had lost traction and came to rest in the thick red clay mud. What a mess! There was no way we could start unloading the truck at that distance. Everything we owned would be full of mud. We had moved to a dead-end road, with only three houses past our driveway. We saw one car drive by and the elderly man waived. I remember thinking how nice the people seemed here. To our absolute delight, the man who had driven past in his car, returned to our yard driving his farm tractor. He said "Come on Yankee, lets pull that truck up to the house." That farmer lived at the end of our dead-end road and not only did he come to our rescue that day, but became a faithful friend and grandfather-figure for our family. To this day, Fred's friends in White Pine still call him Yankee. Friends have actually come to White

Pine, not knowing our address during those early years and been given directions straight to our house, just by asking for Yankee.

While moving things into the house, I stopped to take a break and look out the laundry room window. There were those mountains with the look of rippled and folded velvet. The sun was shining bright on the mountains with shadows in other areas, making it look like areas of bright and dark velvet. It was breath taking. As I looked at this awesome creation, I started to cry over the beauty and was over-whelmed that God would place us here in the midst of all this beauty. I had never seen anything so beautiful in my life and this was where we lived now. Jessica came around the corner just at that time and said, "Mommy, are you sad?" I smiled the hugest smile I could muster up and said, "No, baby, Mommy is so happy that I am crying happy tears."

I love to tell the story now, how God brought us to White Pine, Tennessee. When people realize that you moved from New Jersey, they always ask what brought you to Tennessee. People are always expecting the response to be a job transfer or moving to be near family. People never understand why someone would pack up and leave the home you have always known, your family and friends, just over a *feeling*. I love to share how God totally humiliated me and my navigational skills by not allowing me to drive to Morristown that day. How silly I felt having to tell Margaret, that we "could not get there from here." And most of all, I love that sweet memory of Margaret telling us "We will look in White Pine, since that is clearly where God has plans for you." Margaret has remained our dear friend over all these years and I love her for being a faithful servant of the Lord.

Matthew 7:13

"Enter through the narrow gate, for wide is the gate and broad is the road that leads to destruction, and many enter through it."

Chapter 3

Being in the right place at the right time

✝

My first job when moving to Tennessee in 1992 was on the 7 PM- 7 AM shift at a hospital based Rehabilitation center. I had worked in only one hospital my entire nursing career prior to moving to Tennessee. I had worked at the same hospital for 16 years. I had known everything about that hospital. Now, I was working at a new place, and feeling a little out-of-place. The patients were mostly older adults with strokes and fractured hips getting rehab so they could return home. I had never done anything with Rehab before, so this was entirely new for me. It was important that the patients practice the skills they were shown in the rehab gym during the day. Sometimes it meant that a stroke victim would need to learn to use their non-primary hand to eat supper, since the primary hand wouldn't work for them any-more. Putting their clothes on and off became a frustrating task for the patients using the new skills they were being taught.

Assisting these residents caused me to develop more patience. No longer could I just do things for them. In rehab it was most impor-tant that they learn to perform these tasks for themselves, so they could return home and be independent. It takes a much longer time to allow them to do it themselves, so in doing so, I really got to know my patients well and fell in love with them in the process.

There was also the issue of adjusting to the change in culture. Moving from New Jersey to Tennessee also resulted in a communication issue. Some of the *more country* patients had a thick Tennessee drawl, which I really had to concentrate to understand. There were many times that I would just need to smile and politely ask them to repeat what they were saying. I recall one time when a sweet elderly woman was asking for her *pull-ups*, and after offering her about everything she could pull-up, it became clear that she wanted her house slippers. To this day, I still can't figure that one out. Even the more educated patients that were easier to understand had words I didn't always understand the meaning to at first. One elderly gentleman asked for "some sugar" as I delivered his supper tray. I immediately scurried down the hall to the snack room and returned carrying 2 packs of sugar. He was laughing when

I returned and I soon learnt that wanting "some sugar" in the south, meant that he wanted a kiss. Those first few years, it was common to hear, "you're not from around here are ya?"

I would also need to deal with family members. There were also many times that families would need to be *reminded* not to do things for their loved one, but to allow them to practice the task they were learning. This allowed me to get to know the family members, since most families would visit after work, which was on my shift.

I would see all sorts of emotions from family members. Sometimes I would see guilt from the children who had not visited their mother or father as often as they felt they should have, and now their parent was *like this*. I would hear bitterness, for feeling that they needed to visit more frequently than they wanted to visit, or words of resentment that they would now need to *check on* mom or Dad when they got home. As the nurse, I would shoulder their concerns and comments. I was the sounding board, the non-family member that they could tell how they really felt, without getting judged or condemned. This was both an honor and a burden at times. Never-the-less, there I was for the patients and their family members, as they were going through these life changing times.

Most times I would get a hug and a "thank you" from families as they left with their loved-one on their way home. It was a very satis-fying job, seeing such progress and physical improvement, so patients could be discharged back to their own home.

There was one daughter who would visit her mother every evening. I remember thinking that she must have been a very devoted and committed daughter, who loved her mother very much. After a few weeks, I saw a look in her eyes which really concerned me. It wasn't anything I could put my finger on it was just a very sad and exhausted look. I remember being very busy that night; yet felt that I needed to take the time to speak with her before she left. The Holy Spirit's still small voice told me "it must be tonight." She was always alone, and had never mentioned children or needing to be home at a certain time, so I felt confident that she would take the time to talk with me when I asked her. Not wanting to interrupt her visit with her Mother, I watched as she left her mother's room and started walking toward the exit. I caught up with her in the hallway. I slipped my arm around her back and asked her if she had some time to talk with me. She nodded her head *yes* and her eyes filled with tears, as I took her hand into mine. I took her to an area with less traffic and told her that "God loved her and felt her burden." I told her that I was always there for her and would love to take the time to talk right then.

What came next blew me away. She did need to talk and it was apparently the perfect timing. She must have talked for about 30 minutes about how she was abused by her mother as a child and how she hated her. She talked about how resentful she felt having to take care of her mother and how she was not looking forward to taking her home. The social worker had apparently had a conversation with her earlier that day and told her that her mother had not regained her prior functioning level and was not safe to live alone, so her mother would need to live with her. I remember thinking, *OK, I asked for this.*

I held this sweet lady in my arms and hugged her for the longest time, while not saying a word, yet in the spirit asking God to *give me the words.* The hugs were therapeutic for her, as

God gave me the words to say. I was prompted by the Holy Spirit to tell this sweet lady "God still loves you regardless of how you feel about her mother." She leaned back and looked right into my eyes and said, "I was just thinking that if I couldn't love her, God couldn't love me either." I shared that God's love was unconditional. I shared with her that forgiveness was not about the other person, but something she needed to do for herself. I told her, that when we spoke the words of forgiveness, God would do the rest. I gave her permission not to return and visit her mother until she felt like she wanted to visit. I told her that I didn't expect her to return back to the Rehab center to visit her mother for at least 3 nights and not to feel guilty. I told her "Jesus loves you and wants to know that you love him too." I assured her that her mother's needs were being met, and that she was to take the time off to enjoy herself without feeling guilty. I also shared with her other options and alternate living places her mother could go when she was discharged from Rehab. I asked the daughter what she would most like to see happen. She said she would love to see her mother able to return to her own home. I took her hands in mine and prayed a simple prayer for God to "restore her mother's condition to allow her to live in her own home again."

The daughter returned to the hospital after taking 4 nights off. When she entered the rehab unit that night, she was obviously looking for me. When she saw me in the hallway she gave a huge smile and headed in my direction. She was carrying a small gift-wrapped box in her hands. As she approached me, she held out the gift toward me and said "this is for you." I immediately started my speech about not accepting gifts, but she interrupted mid-sentence. "No, you must take this gift. It's from my heart!" She grabbed me in her arms and hugged me with the tightest hug I had felt in a long time. Then she told me what was on her heart.

She told me that the night, when I had stopped her and made her talk, was indeed the turning point of her life. I recall the words she said, as if it were just yesterday. She said,"I was going home to kill myself that night." I remember thinking... Oh My God! Talk about being in the right place at the right time!

She shared that she had spoken words of forgiveness for her mother that night when she got home, even though she didn't feel like forgiving her mother for all those years of abuse. She said that God indeed had come and done a mighty work as she told Jesus that she loved Him and gave herself totally to Him. This sweet lady had never shared her feelings with anyone before, not her pastor, not her husband, and not her family. She told me that she had "felt condemned" for not loving her mother, since she had always heard the Bible "commanded" her to love her mother.

"Whoa, right there... let's go get a Bible and see what the word of God says." I said. I knew there were lots of Bibles on the unit, so I quickly went to borrow one. I thought the commandment said to 'honor' your father and mother, but I would hate to put my foot in my mouth at this point. Most patients had a Bible in the Rehab unit, so I knew that it would not be difficult to borrow a Bible. Returning with a Bible, I used the concordance in the back of the Bible to find 'Commandments.' I joked with her that I had no idea where those commandments were in the Bible, but we could find them together. I turned to Exodus 20:12. There it was: "Honor your father and your mother, so that you may live long in the land the Lord your God is giving you." She seemed genuinely surprised that it did not say Love your father and mother. Although we are to love all people, she had been confused about what this commandment actually said.

"Enough of that," I said, "You can determine for yourself the difference between love and honor. You may require the use of a dictionary." I reached for the gift that I had left sitting on the counter at the nurse's station. I unwrapped the gift, and lifted the top of the box off to reveal its contents wrapped in tissue paper. It was the most dedicate candy dish in the shape of a heart with roses engraved all around. "I will cherish this," I told her hugging her tightly.

She told me that she was now strong enough to actually tell her mother that she forgave her for all the abuse and she knew that she needed to tell her mother that Jesus loves her. As she headed down the hall toward her mother's room I could feel Jesus *smiling.*

As she left that night, I watched her walk down the side steps from the rehab unit to her car, thinking the difference we can all make in this world, when we ask God to *use us.* I often prayed "use me today Lord" on the way to work as I was driving. After that day, I prayed that prayer every night. "Use Me today Lord." If we are obedient to allow God to use us... think of what we can collectively accomplish.

I never saw that sweet daughter after that night. Her mother was discharged the next day and the daughter had no need to return to the hospital. The patient's chart was sitting at the nurse's station when I arrived to work that next night and I opened it to see to where the mother had been discharged. She had been discharged to her own home with assistance to be provided by home health services. I stood there smiling, knowing that the daughter was smiling somewhere too.

Praise God! Use me Lord.

1 Chronicles 5: 20

"... He answered their prayers, because they trusted in him."

Chapter 4

Changing Churches

†

Within a two year period of moving to Tennessee, I was once again feeling that stirring in my spirit. As was our custom, when we moved to Tennessee we immediately started attending a Baptist Church. The church was small with a hand-full of families attending. The congregation was mostly older adults, with only a hand-full of children that David and Jessica could socialize with during church. While attending this church, both our children received Jesus as their personal savior during Vacation Bible School on July 20, 1993 and were baptized on October 24, 1993. They were baptized on the same month and day that Fred and I had received Jesus as our personal savior years earlier. I believe this was no coincidence. God was showing us how faithful He was, to answer our prayers that our children would also receive Jesus as their personal savior. Fred and I had tithed for several years prior to moving to Tennessee, so of course we had continued to tithe while attending this small Baptist church.

The church had the custom of taking the offering early in the service, counting it immediately and entering the total offering on the board in the front of the church. Each Sunday, I would feel disheartened to see that total offering listed as only a few dollars more than we had given. I would look around the church and count the adults sitting there, realizing that if they had each given just one dollar, it would have been more than the listed amount on that board.

When I felt this stirring in my spirit, that there was something *more* I realized this would mean changing churches. I didn't feel so connected to this church that leaving would break my heart, yet I wondered how they could possibility pay the bills without our contributions.

As the stirring continued for several weeks, I discussed what I was feeling with Fred. During this discussion with Fred, I could see that he was uncomfortable with another change. There had been so much change in the last two years, I'm sure that he was longing to remain at that small Baptist church. Again I prayed, "God, if this is what we are supposed to do... you tell him." I would look at various churches around the area, wondering where God would want us to go. I knew that God was making changes in our lives and that He would soon show us which church we were supposed to attend.

Within a few weeks we were on vacation in Panama City Beach, Florida. Since we always enjoy visiting different churches on vacation, upon our arrival we searched for a local church to attend the next morning. The name Faith Christian Family Church on Back Beach Road caught our attention. Arriving the next morning we were welcomed into the church as if we had attended that church our entire lives. I could feel that the church was *alive*. My spirit *bonded* spirit-to-spirit as I met several people. As the worship music played I felt my spirit soar. I was feeling something I had never felt before. As I asked God what I was feeling, I heard very clearly, "you are feeling me. I am here." Visiting that church made me thirsty for more of what God had to offer. After the service I spoke with a woman who was about my own age. She shared that she had previously attended a Baptist church and had also visited this church while on vacation. She said that after feeling the *anointing* she could not return to a *dead* church. So, that was what I was feeling! I was feeling the *anointing.* I knew that feeling was what I wanted and needed. I wanted to *feel* the Holy Spirit, and that was what the anointing was all about. That night in our condominium, Fred and I prayed for God to show us the church we should attend in Tennessee. We both wanted more. We had tasted more.

A few nights after we had returned home from vacation, I had a dream that we were driving through our small town and that we turned left at the only traffic light in town and went to church. In the dream there was a small church on the right side of the road. When I awoke, I told Fred about the dream. Fred reminded me that there was a huge Baptist church on the road, yet that church was on the left side of the road. God had clearly shown me the church was on the right. Fred and I went for a ride in the car to see what church was on the right side of that road. As we turned left at the only traffic light in town, we passed the hardware store and drove a little further. The only building on the right side was a community building. I remember feeling that I *knew* the church was supposed to be right there! But, where was it? How odd. As we turned the car around and headed back past the community building, I saw a sign. The sign said a church was meeting there. Halleluiah! There was a church there! Fred agreed that we would attend that church the following Sunday. I was wondered about the church the remainder of the week. The newspaper that week also listed the new church and stated it was non-denominational. I had no idea what that meant.

A new Church

Sunday morning, as we drove into the community building parking lot, we were amazed at all the people parking and going into the building. There were lots of kids too. I was excited about that, since kids are a sign of a growing church. As we walked to the door, I remember thinking; we aren't going to know anyone here. As the door opened, the first person we saw was David's teacher. Linda was not just a "teacher," she was a dedicated and loving special education teacher, who had made David realize he was exactly how God had designed him to be. In the two years that Linda had worked with David, his self esteem had grown and he was proud of his accomplishments. There she stood! She welcomed us into the church and immediately introduced us, as her good friends, to the pastor and other members. What a nice feeling! Again I felt that *spirit-to-spirit* bonding that I had felt in that Florida church we had visited while on vacation.

We sat down and I immediately felt like we were meant to be here. The music started and the live band consumed every sense in my body. This was like nothing I had ever experienced before. These were not church hymns sung with a church organ; these were up-beat songs, like the ones I had been listening to on the Christian radio station. We were singing *to* our Heavenly Father instead of just singing about Him. There were two guitars, drums, and four singers. People really seemed to be getting into the praise music and they were raising their hands as I had seen people raise their hands at the church in Florida. I stood there watching and wondering why they raised their hands. What was the purpose of raising their hands? I would surely have to know why.

There was one point in the service that people had gone forward to receive prayer. I was used to people getting prayed for, but here hands were placed on their foreheads as they prayed for them. While being prayed for, some people were falling onto the floor. I had seen this happen on TV, but I had always thought they were pushed over. Being close in the service, I could see that they were not pushed over. They were being touched gently and were falling over. They appeared to be very content lying on the floor as if enjoying some type of peace. I needed to learn about that. In my spirit, I knew I was here to learn more, and was I ever!

The praise music lasted a whole hour, before the preacher ever started to talk. That hour went by so quickly, that I never realized the time. I had really enjoyed church for the first time in my life. I couldn't wait to get in the car after service, so our family could discuss what we had just experienced. I was hoping that everyone was feeling like I was. I had been watching Fred and the kids during the worship time and they all seemed to enjoy it.

We were all excited talking in the car about what we had just expereinced. David and Jessica were asking questions that I could not answer. I said, "I just don't know, but since God has brought us here, He's obviously showing us something new. We will learn together."

We returned the second Sunday and I told Fred that I wanted to sit in the second row, so I could see and hear better what was going on. It was not a problem, because the kids also wanted to be closer to hear what was going on when people fell down. Sitting in the second row soon became our regular seats. We soon learned that when people went forward for prayer, it was the power of the Holy Spirit that caused them to fall in the spirit. People were being healed by the Holy Spirit of various ill-nesses and diseases when they went forward for prayer. I was in awe of the Holy Spirit at work and wanted to learn as much as possible about this.

Abigail was a gentle spoken Christian lady at the church and I enjoyed talking to her. I felt like I could ask her any question and she would answer openly without making me feel foolish for not having known the answer. I had received Jesus as my personal savior on October 24, 1984, yet had never heard about the baptism of the Holy Spirit. She talked to me about the baptism of the Holy Spirit and prayed with me to receive the baptism of the Holy Spirit. That night I told God that I wanted all the gifts that He had to offer, yet I wanted them to be given *directly from Him.*

I knew things were changing for me spiritu-ally. There were times that I would just know what people were going to say, before they said it. There were times that I would look at someone and know what was wrong with them. I would know that they had a sore back, sore knee, diabetes, high blood pressure, or even if they were pregnant. This did not happen all the time, but only when God chose to allow me to see things.

As we continued to attend this church for several months, I finally got the nerve to go forward for prayer. I can't recall what ailment I was needing prayer for at the time, but it was my opportunity to find out first hand what this falling down stuff was all about. As I went forward, I remember thinking that I would not let myself fall down. As the preacher's hand touched my forehead ever-so-lightly in prayer, an amazing power serge passed through my body. It was not the type of electric surge that hurts you, but a surge of energy and peace. I remember opening my eyes as I lay on the floor thinking, how did I get down here? As I was assisted to my feet, I felt like I had awakened from an 8 hour rest. I was full of peace and felt like I could float with joy. Wow! That was the Holy Spirit! I had just met the Holy Spirit in a very personal way!

As I grew in knowledge, I started learning about the gifts of the spirit. I had always learned that these things were from the times of Jesus and not for now. That is not what the Bible was telling me. God is the same yesterday, today and tomorrow. The gifts were for today, we just needed to ask for them. I remember thinking how awesome it would be to have the gift of healing, while being a nurse. God could use me mightily. So I prayed for God to Use Me! I asked God to give me the gifts that He felt I could use to draw people to him. Use me Lord!

One Sunday in church, as people were going forward for prayer, I noticed that the palms of my hands were becoming hot and red. I felt in the spirit that God was telling me that He was giving me the gift of healing. I did not go forward that day, since I felt so timid and unsure what to do. I would need to get some confidence in this area. I would need some practice, since I surely did not want to make a fool of myself.

Practice! Yes Lord that is what I needed. Lord Use me... But let me *practice* first.

2 Corinthians 9:15

"Thanks be to God for his indescribable gift."

Chapter 5

Can you see who's sitting in the chair?

The time had come for me to change jobs. I had been working the 12-hour night shift at the rehab hospital for two years since moving to Tennessee. Although I had felt like it was a good job, I wanted a job with more normal hours and hopefully with increased pay. I saw a position advertised for a Director of Nursing at a local nursing home. I had never been a Director of Nursing nor had I ever worked at a nursing home before.

I submitted my resume and to my delight was called for an interview. As I drove to the nursing home, I remember asking God if He could *use me* there. As soon as I asked that question, I nearly laughed myself off the road. Could He use me there? What a stupid question! God can use me anywhere.

I interviewed twice for that position, which was surely a great sign. I was not surprised when I got the job offer, since I had already felt in the spirit that I would be working there. I was so excited when I went to work there. I wanted to make a difference in nursing homes. They surely had a bad reputation and I wanted God to use me to change how the elderly were treated.

The first 6 months were certainly a challenge. Staffing was a daily issue. People didn't really want to work in nursing homes. It takes a special person to perform the work that they do and enjoy caring for the elderly. It really took me getting to know each staff member individually and showing them love, appreciation and respect, while setting high standards and expectations. While driving to work, I would pray for the staff and residents each day, in addition to asking God to *use me today*. After the first 6 months, staffing had stabilized and I had gotten to personally know each resident and family member.

Each morning, it was my routine as the Director of nursing, to arrive early and make rounds through the facility actually checking on each resident living there. Sometimes residents were sleeping, and there would be no conversation; while there were others who were always awake and looked forward to my early morning visits and hugs.

I enjoyed those early morning rounds and throughout the weeks and months God would give me words of encouragement for particular residents. I knew that I had been called there and that God was *using me* to make a difference in the lives of the elder residents living in that nursing home.

There was one particular lady who always greeted me with a huge smile and announced my name while I was still a few doors away. She was blind and would await the sound of my foot steps. I would hear her voice announcing my visit, "Helena, I hear you coming child." I would often joke with her that I would change my shoes and sneak in on her someday. She was a great Christian woman and she always had a word of encouragement for me. She was a slender black lady who was well up in years. There was no doubt that she loved Jesus, it flowed from her when ever she opened her mouth. I often would ask her if she would like prayer to regain her vision. She would always smile and say something like, "Child, this is not a bad thing. There are worse things. I have Jesus and that's the best thing." Oh, to be so satisfied with your life. She never complained. She was blessed and that is what she told everyone. When asked how she was, she would always start her conversation with, "I am blessed."

One particular morning will remain in my memory forever; she greeted me while I was still a distance off and further down the hall then usual. I could hear her voice calling me to her room while I was still a number of rooms away. The excitement in her voice actually caused me to skip by several rooms, to see what she needed. As I entered her room she was sitting up in her bed with the biggest smile ever. "Good morning Helena… I've been waiting for you." What she said next, I was not prepared for: "Do you see who's sitting in that chair?"

She was pointing to a chair sitting at the foot of her bed in the corner of the room. The chair sat empty. I was considering how I should answer, yet just felt like I should answer straightforward. "Sweetie," I said, "The chair I am looking at is empty. Please tell me what you are seeing." The fact that she said she was *seeing* anything, was in itself amazing.

"Not *what* I'm seeing … but *who* I'm seeing." She answered boldly. "It's Jesus! Can you see him?" No, I could not see him. Gosh, how I wish I could. I looked at that chair with a deep longing to see the face of Jesus! This sweet lady was not confused a day in her life. She was sharp and her mind was totally intact. If she said she could see Jesus sitting in that chair, then Jesus was sitting in that chair. Jesus was sitting just steps away from me, and yet I could not see Him for myself. I walked over to the chair, hoping to feel His presence, yet I felt nothing.

I asked why Jesus had come to visit her today, and she said, "He's come to take me home today." I asked her if she was feeling like she was going to pass away and she said, "No Baby, that's the best part." I asked her what Jesus was doing now, and she looked sweetly toward the chair and said, "Child, He's looking at you and He's smiling."

He was SMILING at me. Jesus was smiling at me! I just stood there in awe of Jesus, in my presence that I could not see for myself. I remember saying to her, that I wished I could see Him too. She responded that it was not yet my time to see Him, but that day would come. She said I had lots of work to do, before it was my turn to see Jesus. I often think about that day and that Jesus was smiling a ME! When does anyone ever have the privilege of knowing that

Jesus is smiling at them? That day changed my life forever and set me on a course to better hear God's voice and do His will. I knew that I had lots of work to do, and need to clearly hear what He wants me to do.

That lovely lady was not ill in any way. Other then being old, her vital signs were fine and she looked perfectly fine that day. Her breathing was regular and she said she didn't have a pain anywhere. After lunch, she took her customary nap. Jesus took her home that afternoon while she was sleeping. What a glorious day!

Someday I will see Jesus face to face for myself. But for now, I know that He *smiled* at me that morning. The day that changed my life forever.

John 14:3

"And, if I go and prepare a place for you, I will come back and take you to be with me that you also may be where I am."

Psalm 27:8

"My heart says to you "seek his face!" Your face. Lord, I will seek."

Chapter 6

Waiting on God to Provide

†

While working at the nursing home as the Director of Nursing, there were many changes and challenges. There were 120 elderly residents that lived there in addition to keeping all the families happy as well. Some days it felt like a responsibility which was impossible, yet on other days, it was a joy and delight to serve them all. It really takes a servant's heart to be a nurse in a nursing home.

When I had first started working there, the Administrator was a young man who was fun and full of life. He was a new Administrator and had not lost the enthusiasm of his youth. He was a joy to work with and committed himself totally to the facility and its residents. Unfortunately, most Administrators lose that characteristic after many years in a nursing home and pressures to keep everything perfect while remaining in budget. As fate would have it, this young man quickly burned out and decided upon another career path. My heart was broken as this meant another change was coming. A new administrator would mean changes yet again, as everyone felt *their* way was the best. So, changes would be coming.

The new administrator was a woman. She was very nice and seemed easy to work with. As a Christian, I never put an advertisement in the newspaper when I needed staff. I would pray and God would provide exactly what I needed and not a minute too late. It was true witnessing of the Christian faith to allow others to see God provide. Waiting on God to provide takes 100% faith.

This new female administrator did not understand *waiting* on God to provide. Her philosophy was to advertise for staffing needs and not be *crazy* about alternate ways to attract staffing. She and I had several conversations about advertising and I had respectfully disagreed, yet agreed that anytime God did not provide, I would allow an advertisement to be placed into the local newspaper to address our staffing needs. At one point I had told her, that if God did not provide the need, I would personally work that open position until a replacement was hired through an advertisement.

Waiting on God to provide was very effective and surely increased my boldness and trust in God to provide. God was always on time and never late. Staffing was always covered and we were never short on any given shift.

One weekend, I needed to go into the facility, after being called about staff issues. That facility visit resulted in four staff members being terminated on a Saturday night. Upon arriving to work on Monday morning, the administrator greeted me at the front door and insisted that I advertise for the open positions immediately, as we were in a critical situation with the four having been terminated over the weekend. I respectfully told her that I had already prayed for God to provide, and in the event that the need was not filled by God by 12 noon, I would call the newspaper to place the advertisement.

It was 8 AM and as I entered my office, I prayed, "Lord, please show her that you will always provide. Please give me more than enough. By 12 noon, please Lord," I went about doing my job duties and didn't think any more about it. Monday mornings were always extremely busy, so I was distracted for three hours and the time passed quickly.

At 11 AM, as I came back to my office, I could see that the lobby was full of people. It looked like a group had gathered for an activity. Outside groups were always coming into the facility to sing or otherwise entertain the residents, so this was not an unusual sight. Within a few moments, the Administrator was at my office, asking me in a very sarcastic tone of voice, if "Your God had provided?" I told her that I would check with the receptionist to see if any applicants had come yet, and reminded her that it was 11 AM, that I still had another hour left. She seemed very annoyed at me. As I walked to the receptionist, the Administrator was following closely behind me. I'm sure that she was expecting to gloat in the results. I asked the receptionist if anyone had come in to apply for clinical positions and she looked at me as if I had lost my mind. She said, "These people are all here to see you. They have all shown up within the last hour and completed applications. They are waiting to be interviewed. You were busy, so I asked them if they could wait and they all said yes." I asked her, "All of them?" I counted around the room and there were 8 people sitting there waiting to be interviewed. Eight! That was twice what I needed.

How awesome is God? Isn't it just like God to give us more then we need and before we need it? That day was an awesome example of God's provision and a powerful witness to the administrator of the facility. I know that God was blessing me for my obedience and standing on faith in His provision. Waiting on God to provide can often be challenging, as it causes our flesh to submit totally to God's timing. We are always trying to *fix* our situation, so waiting on God to provide can seem like an eternity, especially in the *I want it now* society.

Mark 9:23

"If I can?" said Jesus. "Everything is possible for him who believes."

Chapter 7

I ran over the dog

†

When we moved to Tennessee in November of 1992, we knew we would need to add to the family. Having pets is one of the best ways for children to learn responsibility and unconditional love. That first Christmas, each child received a puppy as a Christmas gift from Fred and I. David got a healer. I had never heard of a healer before we moved to Tennessee. David called her "Katie" and she was the most dedicated and loving dog. Katie was a middle sized dog and reddish brown in color. Her coat had a speckled pattern on the legs which made her look like she had freckles. This made David feel special to have a dog with freckles, since David was red headed and also had freckles. I wish I could say that Fred and I had been clever enough to have actually chosen Katie for that reason. David noticed the freckles immediately and was sure that had been part of our plan. Katie was very smart and as I later learned her breed to be an Australian cattle dog. They have in inept ability to bring the cattle in from pasture and also, to my delight, the ability to keep your children in the yard. Katie would circle around in front of their legs to change their direction if she felt they were indeed headed in the wrong direction. It was a wonderful trait to watch. Katie immediately loved each family member and demonstrated her feeling of being responsible for us.

Our puppy choice for Jessica was from the other end of the spectrum, a black Chihuahua. David's dog was purchased from a neighbor for a small amount of money; Jessica's Chihuahua was purchased from a pet store in the local mall. We were told that the breeder had not registered him, so this Chihuahua was only $250. We didn't care if the puppy had any papers, as we only want a pet. We had no intentions to ever breed our newest family member. What a bargain, we thought. He was adorable and Jessica named him "Simon." Simon was to be our 'in-side' dog. From the very start, we wondered why Simon's ears didn't perk upright. We soon came to realize that Simon was not a pure-breed Chihuahua, although he surely looked like one. His ears never did perk upright or flare like that of a pure-breed Chihuahua. Never-the-less, Simon was a member of our family and well loved, even when Simon would make confetti out of the toilet paper, when the bathroom door was left open. Although Simon would tremble like a pure breed Chihuahua when he got excited or cold, our vet told us that he surely was a terrier mix. It really never did matter, since Simon was adorable and loved to snuggle, he fit right into the family.

One Saturday afternoon, I was busy in the house doing housework; much like any busy working mother would do on any given weekend. I had taken Jessica to the church for worship practice earlier and was awaiting her call for me to come and pick her up. The telephone call came from Jessica that worship practice was over, I grabbed my keys and went to the car. David had a friend over and they were busy in the garage. Since David was now a teenager, it was safe to leave him alone for a short time; the church was only about one mile away and I would be back within 5 minutes.

Fred was out and would be returning momentarily as well.

As I hurriedly backed my car out of the garage, I heard a terrible scream. I was unlike any scream I had ever heard. I didn't see anyone around the car, yet thought I better pull the car back forward and look. As I put the car back into drive to pull forward, David came running out of the garage yelling, "No, Don't go forward. You'll run over him again."

I had run over Simon. I had let him outside just before Jessica's call came, and had forgotten he was outside. Getting out of the car, I was shocked to see Simon laying in the gravel driveway in front of my driver's side back tire. Simon was in terrible pain and was yelping. As David and his friend attempted to pick him up, Simon was snapping at them not to touch him. As I bent down on my knees in the gravel, next to Simon, I could see he was dying. He was having trouble breathing and he had blood coming out of his nose, ears and mouth. His eyes were dilated and fixed. He also had bowel movement coming out of his little penis. His hind legs were broken and facing in the wrong direction and I could tell that his bones were shattered. When I picked him up into my arms, I could feel the bones fragments rattling together. He was totally crushed; there was no way this dog could live.

At that very moment, my husband Fred pulled his truck into the driveway. I yelled for Fred to get into my car and drive, so I could hold Simon in the back seat. As David ran out of the house with a blanket, which I could place under Simon, I told him to call the vet and tell them we were on our way with Simon. I got into the back seat of the car, Fred placed the blanket on my lap and I laid Simon on the blanket on my lap.

As Fred drove, I watched Simon struggle to breath, knowing he would be gone before we reached the animal hospital. The animal hospital was about 20 minutes away, and I was sure there was nothing they could do. I sat there with Simon on my lap, thinking how Jessica would feel when she knew I had killed her precious dog. Simon was about four years old now and he was such a special part of our family. Simon would sleep with Jessica every night. Simon would actually tell Jessica that it was time to go to bed. Simon would dart back and forth between Jessica and her bedroom door repeatedly. It was like clock work. Simon knew when it was bed time. I sat there in the back seat blaming myself for being irrespon-sible and not remembering to put Simon back in the house before I got into the car that day. I had never left Simon outside when I left in the car. What had I been thinking?

Then that little voice... the one I had so often heard... the inner voice of the Holy Spirit spoke clearly to me. "I have given you the gift of healing and you wanted to practice. Now it is time to Practice!" Wow! Yes Lord, I can pray healing on Simon. I remember thinking, "What have I got to lose? He's dying." I laid my hands gently on Simon's back and my first words were for the pain to be gone... and Simon let out a gentle moan. I started praying healing over Simon. As I prayed, I could feel my hands become hot. I asked that God would totally heal his little body, in the name of Jesus. I prayed for God to fix his broken bones, to put his intestines back together and fix what ever was causing the blood to come out of his nose, mouth and ears, in the name of Jesus. I asked that God's healing would last many years and that Simon would be Jessica's pet until she was grown and prepared to lose her precious pal, in the name of Jesus. As I was praying with my hands on Simon, I had my eyes closed the entire time, but at one point, after about 5 minutes of praying, Simon licked my hand. Simon licked my hand! It was only then that I opened my eyes and looked at Simon.

Simon was looking straight into my eyes. His head was raised and his eyes were shiny. There was no blood coming out of his ears, nose or mouth. His legs were all facing in the right direction once again. As I gently ran my fingers down his legs, I could feel no shattered pieces of bones. Simon was resting quietly on my lap. His breathing was easy and regular. All the signs that I had previously seen were gone. Simon was healed! As we reached the animal hospital and Fred came around to help me get out of the car with Simon, I told Fred that I had prayed healing over Simon as he drove. I didn't want to seem overly confident to say that Simon was healed. I thought, let's just see the x-rays.

The x-rays showed no broken bones and no internal damage. The Vet said that she thought his back leg was slightly out of the socket, and she gently pushed it back into place. Simon was kept at the animal hospital over night just to be sure that he was fine. When I picked him up the next morning at the animal hospital, he was fine. Praise God! To God be all the Glory and praise for healing Simon that day.

Simon was definitely a revived dog after that day. Not only was Simon healed, but he was obviously able to see into the spirit realm. I had often heard that babies and animals could see into the spirit realm, yet I had never experienced any *evidence* to support that theory. Jessica and I were sure that Simon was seeing angels in the house. Simon would frequently follow *someone* with his eyes. One time while

Fred and I were alone in the living room one evening watching television, I saw that Simon was distracted looking at someone at the center of the room. This time, Simon seemed much more excited then usual. I got Fred's attention, so he could also watch Simon. Simon was wagging his tag and looking up, as if extremely joyful to see someone. Then, Simon stood on his back legs and fanned his front legs up and down, as if wanting the person to pick him up, or if that person were speaking excitedly to him. This was the only time that Simon stood on his back legs and appeared wanting to be picked up by a spirit person; he obviously loved the person we could not see. I have often wondered if Simon was actually seeing Jesus that day in our house. This was a common day-by-day occurrence, Simon would look off, as if seeing someone and wag his tail, and we had all come to know there was what we felt were

heavenly angels in the house and felt comforted in the fact. One day while Jessica and
I were alone in the living room, Simon again
was distracted looking at someone. I said to
Jessica, I remember hearing that the angels
were there to minister to us, and I thought they
may also take direction from us. I said out loud,
"angel, please walk over and stand in front of
the fireplace." To my amazement, Jessica and
I watched Simon's eyes follow someone from
the center of the living room to the front of the
fireplace, as Simon wagged his tail the entire
time.

Simon lived a long life. He was 16 years
old when his health started failing him. He was
uncomfortable and wanting to be held all night,
since his hearing and vision were about gone.
It was a hard decision to put Simon to sleep, yet
ultimately it was the right decision for Simon.
Jessica had gotten married and now lived in

her own house. Simon still lived with Fred and I, as it was the only home Simon had ever known. The prayer that I prayed over Simon in the back seat of my car that day had indeed come to pass. Not only was he totally healed that day, but Jessica was now 24 years old and prepared to lose her precious pet. Praise God! To God be all the glory! Amen!

John 14:12-13

"I tell you the truth, anyone who has faith in me will do what I have been doing. He will do even greater things than these, because I am going to the Father. And I will do whatever you ask in my name, so that the Son may bring glory to the Father."

Chapter 8

Calming the sea

✝

When Fred and I had first gotten married, we lived in New Jersey; so of course, we would travel to the New Jersey beaches during the summer to enjoy the beach. We would usually take a few days and spend time on the New Jersey beaches with friends or family. The New Jersey beaches are on the east coast and the waves usually come into the shore very rough. I had always had a fear of the waves from the times I was a child and would never venture out into the waves without having someone to hold my hand. I didn't just want to be near someone that I trusted, I wanted them to actually be holding my hand the entire time I was in the waves. So, that was Fred's job! He had married me so he was now responsible to hold my hand in the waves. Sounds a bit childish, yet Fred really did enjoy hand-holding in the waves, and never once complained about having that assignment.

I was able to swim and was actually a pretty good swimmer. I had not learned to swim until I was 12 years old, when my parents had an in-ground pool installed in our back yard. The decision to install the pool was very aggressive on my parent's part since my father was the only one in our family who could swim. The goal was that my brother and I would learn to swim, which actually was what happened. My brother and I learned to swim the first year the pool was installed. My Mother could not swim. She had a terrible fear of the water. As Mom spent time in the shallow end of the pool with my brother and I, she finally had courage to float around the pool in an inflated tire tube. She really loved that tube, as it allowed her to float around the entire pool including the deep end without fear. As Mom built up more courage, she purchased a bathing suit with inflation built-in around the waist. Mom started swimming with the bathing suit with the inflation built-in and increased her confidence. The bathing suit with the built-in inflation actually allowed her to move her arms and legs for real swimming. My brother and I were very proud of Mom for her swimming. We encouraged her to swim with us every time we went into the pool. By this point my brother and I were very good swimmers. We could drive off the diving board and swim down to the deep end of the swimming pool to gather weighted rings, which we had thrown into the pool as a game. I had a great lung capacity and could hold my breath while swimming around the entire perimeter of the pool. One summer afternoon while my brother, Mom and I were in the pool, we convinced my Mom that she should try to swim without that inflatable bathing suit. She had been swimming so well, that she should put on a regular bathing suit and try swimming in the shallow end of the pool. We were both excited when she swam back and forth repeatedly in the shallow end of the pool without putting her feet down to touch the bottom of the pool. Mom did this for several days before we convinced her to try swimming the length of the pool, while staying close to the edge. If she got tired she could grab onto the side. Mom did that. She swam back and forth along the longest length of the pool, swimming over the deep end without ever having to grab onto the side of the pool for support. She was swimming well and we were so proud of her. The very next day, we went back into the pool and Mom started swimming back and forth across the long end of the pool again. I was swimming next to Mom allowing her to stay next to the side of the pool, as I swam across the deep end. All of a sudden, without any warning, I was being pushed under the water. Without warning, I had not had the chance to even take a breath of air before going under the water. I had been pushed under with no air in my lungs. I knew it was Mom pressing down on me, and the harder I tried to swim up or down to get away from her, the harder she held me down. I felt panicked as I had no air and wasn't sure if my brother was seeing what was happening to me. I remember asking God to help me. Then all of a sudden, my brother was in the pool next to me. He was moving around quickly in the water. I couldn't see what he was doing, but I knew I still had the full pressure of my Mother pushing me down. I thought I was going to die that day, as I lost all ability to push or fight back and I could feel my body going limp. Finally, I was pulled to the surface of the water by my brother. I could see my Mother hanging onto the side of the pool crying. She was repeating over and over, "I am so sorry, I am so sorry…" I had almost drowned that day, as my Mother lost her confidence while swimming. She had grabbed onto me for support and apparently couldn't help herself, as she struggled to keep her own head above the water, she pushed me under. My brother had struggled to release her grip on me. He said that he actually had to hit her hard several times before he could finally pry her hands off of me and put them onto the side of the pool. I thank God for my brother that day and his saving my life. I had always enjoyed having an older brother, but that day I was the most grateful. I was about 14 years old when that happened and he was about 17 years old. If he had been any younger, he would probably not have had the strength to save my life. Looking back on that day, I know that was an attack from the enemy. I am sure it was his goal to actually kill me that day. At any rate, I'm sure that is where my fear of those big waves came from.

When our children were young, we often enjoyed beach vacations. We have always enjoyed the sand, sun and water, so the idea of spending a week on the beach was always a "happy thought," as my daughter often said. Our idea of a perfect beach vacation was to rent a condominium on the beach in Florida either on the west coast or on the pan-handle. The beach on the west coast and pan-handle of Florida was always calm and less crowded and the waves were also milder. I did not enjoy waves knocking me over, nor did I want to worry about the children getting caught-up in a huge wave or strong under-tow. When the children got older, they wanted to try a beach on the east coast. They had never experienced the big waves and wanted to try it out. Fred and I agreed that we would plan a vacation for a beach on the east coast. Our vacation was planned on the beach in Virginia on Virginia Beach the summer of 1995. On this particular vacation, we were on the beach and headed into the waves, when we decided that Fred would stay with our son and I would stay with our daughter. We had planned to remain close together, yet as the waves pushed us back and forth, we gradually got further and further apart from each other. Fred and my son were out further in the water riding on the waves, like guys do. My daughter and I were not out in the water as far; we were actually in the place where the waves roll hard and there is more under-tow. I realize now, that had we gone out just a little further, it would have been less stressful and less tiring. That is where we were at the time, right in the wildest section of the rolling of the waves into the beach. The waves were coming in stronger and stronger; I had all I could do to hold myself up. My daughter was right next to me, and I was holding onto her hand trying to keep her calm and upright. I had never told her the story of my Mother nearly drowning me when I was about her age, as I didn't want her to have any fear of the water. She had learned to swim when she was only two years old and she was an excellent swimmer. When the next wave hit us I could no longer hold onto her hand; her hand slipped from my hand. As we both rolled in the wave and we both bobbed back up to the surface of the water, my daughter was crying, "Help me Mommy… make it stop." My baby was crying and scared, I needed to do something immediately. The next wave hit and we both rolled under the surface again, this time bobbing to the surface further apart from each other. I knew that I could not reach her. Another wave about ready to crash on us again. Boldness came over me and I yelled at the top of my lungs, "In the name of Jesus, I command you to be still!" The water immediately leveled out flat and the wave that was about to crash on our heads was gone. I grabbed Jessica's hand and ran out of the water as fast as we could. I wasn't sure how long it was going to last and I didn't want to take my time getting out of the water. As we ran through the water, I said to Jessica, "Don't look back, just run." I could feel in my spirit that if we looked back it was a *doubting posture* and the miracle would stop. It was difficult running in the water to the shore and the process took about 2 or 3 minutes to reach the edge of the water. As we reached the shore we turned around to look at the ocean. It was still flat. It was flat and calm. There wasn't a ripple in the water. People all over the beach were looking at the water, I'm sure wondering what had happened to the waves. I held Jessica in my arms and gave her a big hug, and said, "God loves you so much that He calmed the sea." Jessica stood there with her mouth wide open and said, "Mama, you spoke that. You made that happen." "No, baby," I said, "I didn't do that. God made that happen." I laughed and said, "Isn't God Good?" The ocean now resumed its waves and the water was crashing hard against the shore once more. I said, "Thank you God for calming the sea for us to get out." Jessica and I sat on the beach enjoying the sun and in utter amazement of the power we had just seen in the name of Jesus.

When Fred and David came in from the waves, they asked, if we had seen the strange stillness of the water. Jessica told them what had happened and how God intervened on our behalf. From that day, Jessica and I have always joked about our being "God's favorites." When Jessica would get a blessing, she would say, "Well of course, I am God's favorite." When I would get a blessing I would tell her that I was "God's favorite." This has been on-going over the years. When I call her and ask her to pray for me for any particular need, I always tell her she needs to pray, "Since God answers her prayers faster, since she is God's favorite." We laugh about this little game, yet we know… that God does love us. We are the Apple of his eye.

Matthew 8:26

He replied, "You of little faith, why are you afraid?" then He got up and rebuked the winds and the waves, and it was completely calm.

Chapter 9

She had less then 2 weeks to live

✝

In the fall of 1997, I left the nursing home business for a short couple of years to work in home health. In the nursing profession, there are so many options of work environments; one can always make a change when starting to feel burn out. I enjoyed working in home health, as it allowed me to connect to the elderly in their own home environment. It was exciting to see people in their own homes, while getting to know them and their families. I have enjoyed working with the elderly, as they are the most generous and loving people. They have been around long enough to realize what really matters in life. Most of us, the younger generations, are still on the career treadmill allowing life to pass us by, and missing many priceless family moments. I enjoyed traveling from home to home, as it provided me the opportunity to pray and worship God along the way. Living in Tennessee, which is in the *Bible belt*, it is common to have people praying for you, so it was not unusual to hear my elderly clients tell me that they were praying for me as I traveled from home to home. My common practice was to ask my clients if I could pray for them before I left, which was always graciously accepted. It was easy to pray with my clients in their homes, since it was a non-threatening environment with no on-lookers. They were usually home alone or with only one family member present, so it provided me a couple years to pray for people and gain confidence. I had never felt comfortable praying in front of others, so these two years allowed me the time to practice. I was always big on asking God to let me "practice," and over the years God has been most gracious to allow it. I know that God has a sense of humor, and I'm sure has been amused by my insecurities. He will allow me to go just so far, and then pushes me further, to step up to the challenge.

Several months after I had started working in home health, I visited a lovely lady named Dorothy in her home. She was a sweet Christian lady who had been diagnosed with cancer of her throat. The first time I saw her, she spoke of Jesus and His love for us. It was always nice to visit with a Christian, as I always wanted to learn more as she had been through more and experienced more. Dorothy had been raised in a Christian home and had received Jesus as her personal savior at an early age. Dorothy was in the process of having lots of tests done to prepare for surgical removal of her throat cancer. She told me, that regardless of the surgery outcome, she was prepared to meet her maker and was at peace. Sometimes things happen during surgery, if that was the case, she was fine with that.

As I entered her home on a subsequent visit, I knew something was very different. She was not the happy-go-lucky lady I had come to know and love. As I sat down next to her on the couch, she shared with me that the doctors had told her they could not surgically remove her throat cancer. The cancer had wrapped itself around too many blood vessels in her neck, removal was not possible. I held her in my arms and we just hugged for the longest time. There were no words. There was nothing I could say. Her spirit was broken and so was mine. She was not an old lady; she was only in her late 60's. That was too young to know that you are going to die. Not just die, but to die slowly, not being able to eat and drink. She said the doctor reported it would be a very short time, less then 2 weeks, and for her to make arrangements quickly. By this time, she could no longer eat any food and was having great difficultly getting any fluids down her throat. As I left that day, I hugged her knowing it would probably be the last time I saw her, this side of Heaven.

God awoke me the next morning at 3 AM. I had come to realize that when God wakes me at 3 AM, it's going to be a prayer need. I rolled over in the bed, as that still small voice of the Holy Spirit said, "Pray for Dorothy. Pray for her healing." Yes Lord! I will pray. I prayed for Dorothy's healing. It was not a long prayer time, as I rolled back over and easily went to sleep after about 10 minutes. It doesn't take an extended period of time to pray God's healing. I awoke up the next morning knowing that God had a miracle up His sleeve.

As I drove toward work that morning, that still small voice of the Holy Spirit said, "Go to Dorothy's house and lay healing hands on her." I whined; "But God, I'm not scheduled to see Dorothy today, and if I go there now, I'll be late for work." ... Then silence... God? ... Can I go after work today? ... Is that OK? ... God? ... silence... "OK God," I said, "I will go now, I am sorry." I called work from my cell phone and told them I was running late and would be there as soon as I could. Then, I called Dorothy's house and told her daughter that I was coming for an early morning visit, and she said that was fine.

"Lord," I said, "I'm going. I may be slow to get it sometimes, but eventually I do listen. Please tell me what to do when I get there." Then that still small voice of the Holy Spirit said,

"You had practice." Yes indeed, I had prayed healing on the dog. Simon had been dying and now he's fine. "Yes Lord! I will pray healing on Dorothy like I did for Simon," I said, "But, Lord, could you please allow me to do it alone with Dorothy? Just me and Dorothy" ...Silence... "God?" I said. ...Silence... "God?" ... Silence...

When I arrived at Dorothy's house, I had difficulty finding a parking place. Her driveway was filled with cars, so I had to park along the edge of the street near the driveway. I thought, "Lord...there are a lot of people here." As I walked to the door, her daughter greeted me before I even had to knock. She opened the door widely and greeted me with a hug. I told her that I was not there for a home health visit, but a "God said to come" visit. She smiled and said she liked that kind of visit the best! As I entered the living room, Dorothy was seated in her favorite chair and the living room was full of people. The daughter introduced me to everyone in the room, there were six people including two pastors. "Oh Lord," I thought, "What are you doing to me?" We all chatted for about 10 minutes, as I procrastinated, until I realized no one was leaving anytime soon. At this rate, I would never get to work. I needed to do what God had brought me here to do. I needed to complete my assignment now.

I leaned over and spoke to Dorothy, "God told me to come this morning and pray healing, is that OK with you?" Her faint voice said, "Yes." I placed my hand on her throat, and asked God to heal her. I prayed with my hand on her throat for a while and then felt like I was to move my hand to her head and also pray healing there. As I was praying, I could see that the cancer had also spread up into her brain and God also wanted her head to be prayed for. As I prayed, I could feel that the people in the room were also gathering tightly around Dorothy and me, and joining me in prayer. The environment was becoming thick with prayer and my boldness was becoming stronger. I could hear my voice speaking louder and more commanding. Then I heard the Holy Spirit say to me, "Rebuke it, this is something that needs to be rebuked."

In a loud voice with much authority, more authority then I had ever felt before, while holding my one hand on Dorothy's neck and my other hand on Dorothy's forehead I said, "In the name of Jesus I rebuke you." ... The Holy Spirit said AGAIN... I responded and said, "In the name of Jesus I rebuke you." ... The Holy Spirit said AGAIN... I responded and said, "in the name of Jesus I rebuke you." The Holy Spirit said... "It is done."

Dorothy didn't die in 2 weeks! Dorothy's cancer mass on her neck started shrinking immediately and stopped putting pressure on her blood vessels and on her throat. The cancer had withered up. Dorothy started eating normal consistency food and drinking again. Dorothy's strength regained and she no longer needed home health services. She was alive and well, praising God and testifying at her church of God's healing and the miracle in her life. I visited Dorothy for the last time about four months after her healing, as a social visit. She was still praising! To God be all the Glory and Honor. Praise God!

Dorothy went to be with her Lord about a year later. It was a sudden death, as I understand that she choked on a large piece of chicken. It was not a result of cancer returning. The cancer had not re-grown. Her choking death was the result of her not cutting her food properly. I was saddened upon hearing of her death but know I will see her in heaven. I'm sure our conversation will start, *"Remember when…"*

John 14:11

"Believe me when I say that I am in the Father and the Father is in me; or a least believe on the evidence of the miracles themselves."

Chapter 10

Seeing the Holy Spirit on a CAT scan

✝

In the winter of 1997 I started having a lot of coughing. I am not someone who goes to the physician unless I am very sick. I usually like to let the body heal itself, which usually will result in the body becoming stronger. After a few weeks of dealing with the coughing which was not easing with over-the-counter remedies, I finally gave in and made an appointment with my physician. This was a very busy time in my life, as in addition to having a full time job, I was also involved in starting a Christian Pregnancy crisis center. I knew when this project started, that there would be spiritual warfare to contend with, since the enemy would not take kindly to saving babies from certain death. My convictions were strong; I knew that God had his hand on this Christian Pregnancy Crisis Center. On the first visit to my physician in December of 1997, I was told that most likely I had a minor respiratory infection. I was given some medications to ease the coughing and an antibiotic for the infection.

I continued working my 40 hour job in addition to my daily involvement with the planning of the Christian Pregnancy Crisis Center. A supporter for the Christian Pregnancy Crisis Center had donated a house. We were in the process of cleaning and painting the center to prepare for an opening. There was lots of stuff to be done and training to be arranged. Thinking back, although I was so ill at the time, it was a blessed time in my life. The second time that I went to see my physician was in January of 1998. My cough had gotten worse and I was now having difficulty sleeping at night. I was only able to sleep 2-3 hours per night, so I was spending many hours with the Lord in prayer and fellowship. When I would lay my head down on the pillow, I immediately felt like I was going to drown, so I would have to sit back up. This was the first time God had revealed *His* time to me. God had revealed that his timing was not the same as our timing. When I prayed for *His* time, my 2-3 hours of sleep felt like I had actually had a full 8 hours of sleep. Between December of 1997 and February of 1998, I had visited my physician a total of five times. My lungs were always clear when he listened, and although he continued to give me inhalers and respiratory medications, I'm sure that he was thinking I was making a big deal out of a minor problem.

On February 14, 1998 at 4:30 AM I woke my husband, Fred. I had not been able to sleep all night, as my chest and throat were gurgling with fluid. I was so short of breath that I thought I was going to die right there and then. I told Fred that I needed to go to the hospital. Although he did get up and dressed, he kept looking at me like I was not sick. He could only hear a cough, yet he could not feel what I was feeling. No one can fully understand what it feels like to be drowning from within. I knew that this illness was a result of spiritual warfare; I had done everything I knew, to pray and rebuke it. Yet still, here I was without any improvement. In the emergency room at the hospital, the emergency room physician ordered lots of lab work and x-rays. The emergency room physician said that he had not seen a chest x-ray looking so bad in a long time. He said it looked like "Megoblastic pneumonia" and that I was only able to use about 40% of my lungs; he couldn't be sure until the radiologist read the x-rays. I was given an antibiotic injection and sent home with prescriptions for an antibiotic and cough suppressants. Since it was on the weekend, it was not until February 17, 1998 that I received a call from the hospital that my chest x-ray had been read by the radiologist. The radiologist had read the chest x-ray as "Congestive heart failure and pulmonary edema." I was told to immediately report to my physician's office for an emergency Echocardiogram. I was at work when I received the call, trying to push myself, although I felt too sick to work. I immediately left work and drove to my physician's office and had the Echocardiogram. As I drove to my physician's office and was praying, I clearly heard the Lord telling me again that this was "spiritual warfare." I remember saying out loud in the car, "Yes God, I know its spiritual warfare, but I have done everything I know to pray it gone. This is stupid! Are you going to let the enemy kill me?" Then I heard that still small voice of the Holy Spirit, very gently saying, "No my child, I'm not going to let him kill you, but I am going to use this to my glory." Then a peace came over me. I knew it would be fine.

"OK God," I said, "Use me to your Glory."

Over the next two weeks, I had two appointments with my physician for follow-up x-rays and completed my antibiotics without any improvement. During this time, I also witnessed my faith to my Physician, discussed God's provisions and the spiritual gifts. My physician had many questions about the gifts, and I had taken him a taped series on the spiritual gifts. I knew there was to be more... God was still using this illness. Finally, I was scheduled to see a

Pulmonologist (lung Specialist) in Knoxville, TN. I couldn't wait to see that Pulmonologist, as I knew I would start feeling better after that, I was sure. I knew that there was going to be something significant happen when I went to see the Pulmonologist. I knew that God had something more up his sleeve. Frankly, *I was over it,* I had been sick for so long, I just wanted to feel well again. During the weeks of waiting, I continued to work my 40 hour per week job and maintained all my other responsibilities, including proceeding with the Pregnancy Crisis Center training. My prayer remained, "Use me Lord."

On March 4, 1998 I went to see the Pulmonologist. My husband Fred went with me that day. Up until this point Fred had not seen just how sick I was. I'm not sure if he had blinders on or if I had just hidden it so well. At home, I did not complain about feeling so sick, since I really did not want to alarm the children. I surely didn't want them to know that I felt like I was dying. The Pulmonologist's office was located in the medical tower attached to the hospital. We parked the car in the parking garage and took the over-head walkway to the medical building. As we were walking, I could only walk about twenty feet without having to stop and catch my breath. I remember seeing the fear in my husband's eyes for the first time since I had been ill. I remember telling him, that I was going to be OK, that God had told me He would not let the enemy kill me. We must have taken 7-8 rest breaks before we reached the Pulmonologist's office. The pulmonologist knew it was serious as soon as he looked at me. He wanted his own x-rays, so I had additional chest x-rays in his office. Fred and I sat in the examination room waiting for him to view the x-rays. He walked into the examination room and slid the x-rays under the clip on the lighted viewer on the wall. He said, "You are a nurse, have you ever seen a chest x-ray that looks like this with the person still alive?" That question shocked me and caught me off guard. As I looked at the x-ray, I knew that I had never seen an x-ray that looked that bad. The fact that I was alive and had just walked all the way from the parking garage had him totally amazed. He said, "You are only using the top 10% of your lungs. This is impossible, impossible, impossible." As soon, as he said that, I knew how I was to respond! I said, "Nothing is impossible with God." I asked him if he was a Christian, and to that he responded, "Yes." I told him that this was "spiritual warfare," since the enemy was obviously upset about the Pregnancy Crisis Center. I asked him if he had ever seen God's miracles, and he responded, "No." Then I told him that he was looking at a miracle sitting in front of him, since I was indeed alive. The entire time that I was talking and he was responding, he continued to stare at my x-rays clipped onto the lighted board on the wall. After a brief silence, he said, "I have never seen anything like this either." He was pointing to the top portion of my lungs on the chest x-ray films hanging on the wall. There on the x-ray films, in the top 10% of both of my lungs, in the area which I was still able to use, was something he was pointing to. He was saying, "This... right here...look... right here..." His nurse had come into the room now and was also looking at the x-rays hanging on the wall. Then, he said, "It looks like fluffy white stuff." As soon as he said those words, I felt the Holy Spirit tell me, the fluffy white stuff was the Holy Spirit keeping that area open for me to breathe. I spoke it out, "That is the Holy Spirit... that fluffy white stuff is the Holy Spirit keeping that area open so I can breathe." The Pulmonologist turned around quickly and looked directly at me and said, "I think you may be right. I have never seen this before. That may explain it." The Pulmonologist then said, "Would it be OK if I allow others at the hospital to see this x-ray, since it's something I've never seen before?" I responded that it was fine with me, that he allow everyone in his office and in the hospital to see the x-ray of the Holy Spirit. Then the Pulmonologist said, he was going to admit me immediately to the hospital for aggressive treatment. Not only did my chest x-rays show congestive heart failure and pulmonary edema, but the lower 90% of my lungs showed a pleural effusion which would need to be drained by doing a Thoracentesis. But first, he wanted a CAT scan of my lungs, so he could better see what that "fluffy white stuff" was in the upper areas of both lungs. I asked the Pulmonologist if I would see those CAT scan films too and he said, "Oh yes, I will bring them to your room. I wouldn't want you to miss this." So, off I went to the CAT scan Department for an emergency CAT scan. As I was leaving the Pulmonologist's office in my wheelchair, I passed by the main nurse's desk where there were several doctors and nurses looking at my chest x-ray and the "Fluffy white stuff." I heard one nurse say, "I'm betting that is the Holy Spirit and I'm betting the CAT scan will show the same thing." As I left the office, I wondered what a cross section of the Holy Spirit's presence would look like on the CAT scan. Well, we are about to see.

I was in the hospital for five days in the cardiac unit. I had over two liters of fluid drained from my lung cavity when they did the Thoracentesis. As a Registered Nurse, I had assisted physicians with this procedure many times, and knew the risks and benefits of the procedure. I was concerned being on the other end of the procedure as a patient. I knew that a cough during the procedure could cause damage to the lung, so a cough needed to be prevented throughout the procedure. I prayed the entire time, that God would suppress my cough, since I had been coughing constantly. God was faithful and suppressed my cough during the entire procedure. That in itself was amazing. I was able to breathe better after that procedure was completed, although I was still very weak. That first night in the hospital was the first night I had been able to sleep all night in months. I had multiple heart and lung tests performed while I was in the hospital and no one could find any explanation for the condition I had been in upon my arrival. My heart and my lungs were perfectly fine. Every physician, nurse, and technician who I came into contact with during those five days in the hospital, knew about the "fluffy white stuff" on my x-rays and thanked me for allowing my Pulmonologist to share them. I was asked lots of questions about the Holy Spirit and had the opportunity to witness my faith to many staff in that hospital. It indeed had been spiritual warfare. It's amazing what the enemy will do, when you are making advancements for the Kingdom of God! I knew that Pregnancy Crisis Center was going to be a great success, since the spiritual warfare had been so great. God was faithful to save my life and use the event to his glory. Not only had He saved my life, He had also allowed me the privilege of witnessing to the hospital staff about God's presence in our lives, after they receive Jesus as their personal savior. Praise God. To God be all the Glory!

I know that you are wondering about those CAT scan results. The Pulmonologist brought the CAT scan films into my room on the morning I was to be discharged home. Fred and I sat on the edge of the hospital bed waiting for him to arrive, as he had told me he was going to bring the CAT scan films for me to see that morning. When he walked into the room, he said, "These films are been the talk of the hospital. Thank you for giving your permission to share them." He showed me the CAT scan films and the final written report. The CAT scan had shown multiple cross sections of "fluffy white stuff." The cross sections had shown nothing more then what the original x-rays had shown. He said, "The whole hospital is talking about the x-rays and the CAT scan of the Holy Spirit. Everyone is saying that you must have a great call on your life." I asked the Pulmonologist what he thought that "white fluffy stuff" was, and he responded, "My wife and I talked about that just last night. I have never been a strong Christian and I think that God is trying to show me something. I believe that was the Holy Spirit keeping you alive. I believe He allowed His presence to be visible to show me…" He stopped talking and his eyes were visibly wet so I didn't press any further. God was dealing with him on a personal level. This was between him and God. I stood up from the bed and walked to him, hugged him tightly and thanked him for making me feel better. I know that those five days I spent in the hospital affected many lives. Many people need to see physical evidence of all things, especially those working in the healthcare industry. God had indeed allowed His presence to be visible. Isn't that just like God?

If we allow God to USE us, we can work mightily for the Kingdom of God. Life will not always be all sunshine and roses. When we allow God to USE us, we must understand that His ways are not our ways and we must allow God total control. I am still amazed of what God did through me during that time in my life.

Praise God! To God be all the glory! Use me Lord!

Galatians 2:20

"I have been crucified with Christ and I no longer live, but Christ lives in me. The life I live in the body, I live by faith in the Son of God, who loved me and gave himself for me."

Chapter 11

Hearing the Audible voice of God

I left the Hospital on March 8, 1998. I remember Fred driving me home in the car and looking out at the beautiful sunny day. I was praising God for the beautiful day, for allowing me to get well, and return home with to family. There had been many days during my illness that I thought I was going to die. The thought of going home to live with my Heavenly Father was not a bad thought, it was just that I didn't feel that was His plan for me yet. I knew that Fred and the children still needed me, and it was God's plan to allow me to remain here. It was great to be home, although I was shocked how weak I still was. I had been pushing myself for months while I had been ill; I expected to feel great when I got home. My pulmonologist and cardiologist had both told me not to return to work for four weeks, so my body could completely rebound after being so gravely ill. It wasn't until I returned home, that I realized how sick I had been. I didn't have strength to do much around the house. My daughter was very helpful. She helped do the laundry and vacuum the house. Those two tasks were huge for me, as there was no way I could do them yet. Taking care of my own personal hygiene was a day's work alone. After the children would leave for school and Fred would leave for work, I would exhaust myself taking a shower and getting dressed. This weakness went on for two weeks without any significant improvement in stamina. I was getting very depressed during this time, since I had hoped to return to work before the four weeks projected by the pulmonologist and cardiologist. Our finances were not flowing. The time off from work made a huge impact as we got behind on our bills. Each day, I would become more stressed out and depressed. My physical inabilities and the financial affect of my being out of work were grave concerns.

From the first day I returned from the hospital, I was spending hours with God each day. I was watching anything Christian I could find on the TV. I was praying without ceasing and reading my Bible. I knew that I needed to keep my spirit well feed during this time of healing and I knew He was the answer and hope for my finances as well. These four weeks of being totally alone with God also allowed for significant growth in my Christian walk. There were days when I was all alone in the house, while the children were at school and Fred was at work; I would lay face-down on the floor for hours before the Lord. Most of the time, there would be total silence as God ministered quietly, without words, to my spirit, while other times He would speak softly into my spirit and I would know exactly what He was saying. During this time, the voice of the Holy Spirit became clearer then ever before. Hearing God's voice had always been that inner voice, the one you hear in your head. These thoughts you know are not your own.

I remember someone explaining that hearing the voice of God was like singing *Happy Birthday* in your head. I could really relate to that explanation. That was just like how it was for me. The voice was clear yet you knew it was not your own thoughts or words. It was the divine voice. I just knew, that the more I heard it, the easier it became. During that time while

I was off from work and healing my body, the voice became stronger and easier to hear. The small still voice of the Holy Spirit was getting clearer, more consistent, and more frequent. I would wake up each morning and say, "Good morning Holy Spirit." I had read a book written by Benny Hinn 'Good morning Holy Spirit' and was convicted in my spirit to say those words each morning. The more I said those words every morning, the better that day would be for me physically. I would have more energy and I knew that God was working mightily in my life. Those four weeks with God were the spiritual growth that I needed. God was revealing his presence in a way I had never felt before. I could feel His presence in me, on me and all around me. I felt protected and loved like never before. He was showing me His love and I was feeling it.

During this time God was showing me that He was going to use me mightily for the Kingdom, since I was a willing vessel. God was showing me visions of what lay ahead. I know that He was leading me to bring many people to Christ. In one vision He showed me a huge field full of white flowers. The Holy Spirit said, "The Harvest is ready. Others have planted the seeds and you will harvest." In another vision: I saw people pressed tightly against each other being herded forward. They could not see where they were headed. They were happy and content. In the vision, I was watching from overhead, so I could see where they were headed. They were headed to a cliff. Once they were close enough to see the cliff, it was too late to stop, the pressure from the crowd behind them, pushed them over. Below the cliff was a huge fire and I knew that it was hell. People were being pushed beyond their control into that fire.

Every so often, one person would be plucked from the crowd and added to the Kingdom of God. The number of people being plucked out was nothing compared to the great number of people being pushed over the edge of the cliff into the fire. As I was allowed to look closer, I could see that people in the crowd were sitting in wooden pews. They were sitting in church pews, being pushed over the edge of the cliff into the fires of hell. The wood from the church pews were actually feeding the fire and making it hotter. I asked God, "Why are they in church pews?" The answer was shocking. God told me that there were many people going to hell that were in church. They didn't know that they were going to hell. They thought they were right with God. God made it very clear. He told me, "Tell my church, if they don't remember the day of their salvation then it didn't happen. They must say the words for themselves. No one can do it for them." Over and over, I heard, "Tell my people. Feed my sheep." I knew that the enemy was lying to people and making them think they were saved, falsely believing it was acceptable for someone to just *pray over them*, yet they had not personally said the words to ask Jesus to be their personal Savior. That it was a lie from the enemy.

The next Sunday in church, I told my pastor I had a word for the church. I spoke the words that God had given me. "If you don't remember the day of your salvation then it didn't happen. Do you remember the day? Do you remember saying the words, asking Jesus to be your personal Savior? Ask your loved ones... do they remember?" I told about the vision God had given me with the cliff and the fire in hell below. It was a very emotional word, and I had trouble speaking, as the conviction was so heavy. There were lives on the line. My heart was breaking for the people being pushed over the cliff and into the fires of hell.

The following Sunday, one of the men who attended the church came over, hugged me and thanked me for the word from God I had given the previous Sunday. Immediately after church the previous Sunday, he had gone to his Mother's home. She was almost 90 years old and had been a Christian all her life. She still had her memory intact and was able to recall every event in her life. She was not forgetful although she was well up in age. When this man asked his Mother, if she could remember the day that she had asked Jesus to be her personal Savior, she could not remember the day of her salvation or saying any words her-self to ask Jesus to be her personal savior. She shared how "She just knew." This man had the privilege of leading his Mother in saying the sin-ner's prayer that day and I rejoiced with him in her sweet salvation. This woman had lived her entire life with that lie from the enemy that she was "OK." That lovely lady has since passed away. At her funeral, it was joyous to remember that day and know that she was in Heaven with Jesus. I couldn't help but think "it almost didn't happen!"

When God is feeding you and growing you in His ways, there is going to be spiritual warfare along the way. One day, after I had been home for about three weeks, I awoke feeling terrible. I felt more terrible then I did at the height of my illness and didn't feel like I could get out of bed. I didn't recognize this as an attack from the enemy. Looking back now, I should have rebuked it and made myself get out of bed. Yet, that morning, I did not do or say anything. I just laid there feeling sorry for myself. Now, I know what you are thinking! I was alone with God for weeks and still didn't recognize this as an attack. NO! I did not recognize this as an attack from the enemy. I laid there feeling like I was going to die. Frankly with all that I had been through, I was laying there in that bed, feeling like it was OK to just die. I had been through so much; I didn't have anything else to give. I remember laying there in that bed actually saying out loud, "Lord, please just let me die. I'm ready to come home now."

I had dozed back off to sleep, when I was awakened by a loud voice. It was a very loud deep man's voice. It was deep like a roaring river. The voice reminded me of the sound of Niagara Falls in New York State. If you have ever been there, you know the loud roar of the water. Only one word was said, "Gouw-el." It is difficult to even write the word that I heard. I can still hear the word in my memory. To this day, I can't be sure if the first letter should be a "C" or a "G." The loud roaring sound in the voice was amazing, and the roaring could have made the "C" sound like a "G." I jumped up and out of the bed. The voice was loud and it was a word I had never heard before. It was not an English word, yet I immediately knew it meant "arise." The voice was firm and commanding. I immediately left the bed room to check the house. There was no one in the house. There was no one in the yard. I looked up and down the road. There was no one anywhere. I knew in my spirit that it had been God, yet my flesh was looking around to check. It had been God! He was telling me to get out of bed. It was telling my spirit, that he was not granting me permission to just lay there and die. ARISE! He had told me to "ARISE." I apologized to God for wanting to just give up that day. I recommitted myself to allowing him to USE me to the glory of the Kingdom.

That was the last day that I felt sick. The next morning I woke up feeling totally well again. I knew that I had heard the audible voice of God. It would be days before I could share the event with anyone. Each time I started to talk about it, I would be overcome with sobbing and could not speak. When I was permitted to speak about the experience, God had warned me that not everyone would be prepared to hear this word. It is only by permission of the Holy Spirit that I am adding this into the book.

Hebrews 13:8

Jesus is the same yesterday and today and forever.

Chapter 12

She prayed for a Bible

✝

One Wednesday evening as I was driving home from work, I felt compelled to stop at a Christian book store. As I pulled into the parking lot, I was asking myself, why I had stopped. As I sat in the parking lot, I really could not think of anything that I had wanted or needed to buy as we were carefully watching our finances at the time. Yet, I felt like I was supposed to go inside. "God, is that you?" I said, as I walked to the door of the store. As I walked through the store, looking at the various items on display, I was still asking God, what He had in mind. I suddenly felt like we were playing a game. "God," I thought, "Tell me when I'm getting hot." Remember the childhood game, where someone would say "you're getting hot" when you were getting closer to the items or they would say "you're getting cold," if you were headed in the wrong direction. I was walking through the store, waiting for God to give me a clue as to why I was there. Maybe I was there for someone who worked there, or maybe a shopper. As I looked around, I didn't notice anyone needing assistance, looking upset, or having any sense of someone's personal need.

As I walked past the Bible section, that still small voice of the Holy Spirit said, "Buy Debbie a Bible." "Well, Hello God! I've been waiting to hear from you," I said. "Thank You. But, why would I buy Debbie a Bible? She already has one." Debbie was the home group leader of the church home group that we attended. I loved Debbie and she had become very special to me. I would do anything for Debbie! But a Bible? Why does she need a new one? She always uses her Bible during home group and she had never mentioned anything negative about her Bible or wanting a new one. Debbie and I had become very close, so I would expect she would have said something about wanting a new Bible. Again... the still small voice of the Holy Spirit said, "Buy Debbie a Bible." "Yes Lord," I said, "I will buy Debbie a Bible." I started looking at the King James versions, since I knew that was the version she currently had, and seemed to enjoy reading that version. I looked through the various Bible styles in the King James Version, but I kept feeling like that was *wrong.* Each time that I would pick up a NIV version, I felt a peaceful feeling. I would pick up another King James Version, feel that it was *wrong*, then pick up another NIV version and feel peaceful. Yes, I think I'm supposed to get the NIV Version. I started looking at the various styles of NIV Bibles, and felt like I was supposed to get the burgundy colored Bible. Burgundy looks nice and I'm sure that Debbie will like that. I was holding an imitation leather burgundy NIV Bible in my hand as the final selection, when God spoke, "The best! Get her the best with her name." I put down the imitation leather burgundy NIV Bible and picked up the real leather burgundy NIV Bible. The cost was significantly more for the real leather Bible, and I was not sure if, with taxes, I could afford that Bible. The amount that I had in my pocketbook was close. It would be very close. As I walked to the cashier, I was hoping that I would not be short on cash. I was praying to myself, "God please provide. I am being obedient, so please provide." She lady at the register said a name imprint on the front of the Bible was included in the price and asked the name I would like printed. I asked her to ring it up and allow me to pay first. I surely didn't want to have a name printed on a Bible that I couldn't afford. How would that look? When she totaled the order and added the sales tax, I had enough to buy the Bible. As I paid for the Bible, and she handed me back a few coins as change which was all I had left. I only had change left. Praise God! I had enough. Isn't it just like God to always leave a remainder? Praise God! After I had paid, I told the cashier the name that I wanted printed on the front cover of the Bible. As she started to walk away, I heard the Holy Spirit say, "DOVE." I asked the lady if she also had a dove, to imprint with her name and she said she did. So, then, let's print the name with a dove. Would that be an extra charge? No, there would be no extra charge. I was standing there feeling totally awesome. I had heard God's clear directions for each part of the Bible selection: NIV version, burgundy color, leather, name imprint and a dove. I only hope that Debbie will be as excited about this Bible as I am. Tonight is church night, so I will hurry home now and wrap her Bible so I can give it to her tonight.

As I was driving home, I felt like I was supposed to drive directly to Debbie's house and give her the Bible. Without wrapping it up? Really, God, now? I was going to see Debbie soon at church tonight. It would only be about 2 hours and I would see her at church. Yet, never-the-less, if you say now, so be it. Let's go straight to Debbie's house now. As I pulled into her driveway, I was thinking what a busy time of the night this would be for her, as she cooked to feed her family prior to going to church. As

I walked to the door, I hoped that she wouldn't be upset by my unannounced arrival. Debbie opened the door with her usual smile and said "come on in." I apologized for not calling first and handed her bag from the Bible book store. I apologized for not wrapping it, but said God would not let me delay giving it to her. She laughed and said, "Isn't that just like God?"

As Debbie opened the bag she started crying. "It's my Bible… it's my Bible… the one I've been praying for." By now she had opened the box and removed the Bible from the box. She was holding the Bible to her chest while sitting on the floor. When she had opened the bag and saw that it was a Bible, she had crumbled to the floor. She sat there in the middle of her kitchen floor praising God! When she finally stopped crying, she told me that she had been praying for a Burgundy NIV version leather Bible with her name on it with a dove too. She sat there for the longest time, on the floor, praising God for his faithfulness.

I asked Debbie, why the new Bible had been so important to her, since she had never mentioned it to me, ever. Debbie said that her first marriage was a very controlled by her husband. Way back then, she had wanted a NIV Bible and he refused, saying that she could only have a King James Version Bible. The name that was printed on the front of that old Bible, which was all she had to use, had her old married name. She said that every time she opened that Bible she was reminded of her divorce and the fact that she wasn't permitted to have a NIV version Bible. She was now married to the most precious Christian man, and didn't need any reminders on the one book that she reads everyday. Times were tight and she could not afford to go buy a new Bible. She had prayed to God to provide the exact

Bible she was holding in her hands. She had gotten everything she had prayed for... God had provided... including the DOVE. She kept saying," I even got the dove!" Praise God! To God be all the Glory! When we allow God to *use us*, lives can be changed and prayers can be answered. I thank God for using me that day to bless Debbie. I felt more blessed that day, than I could ever imagine. Use me Lord! Praise God! To God be all the Glory!

Mark 11:24

"Therefore I tell you, whatever you ask for in prayer, believe that you have received it, and it will be yours.

Chapter 13

My Grandfather's salvation... the greatest gift

†

My Grandfather, whom I lovingly called "Papa," was my mother's dad. I had grown up living in the house beside my Papa and Nana. Our homes were probably just 1000 feet apart, yet due to the ridge of a hill, we could not see from one house to the other. This allowed a sense of closeness with allowing a sense of privacy as well. Our school bus stop was at the top of that ridge that separated the two houses, which allowed Nana to keep a watchful eye on us as we waited for the bus to arrive. I would spend many hours at their home, which really gave me an opportunity to know them both. Nana had a gentle spirit and was soft spoken most of the time. She had always been a stay-at-home mom and was great in the kitchen. She made the most delicious home-made bread. I could always smell her bread baking and I would follow the irresistible aroma to get a slice of hot bread with her home-made strawberry jam piled on top. She was always showing and telling me about baking, as she was a natural teacher and loved to pass along her "tricks of the trade." Nana lacked self-confidence, since she had not completed her education. I believe she had gotten as far as the sixth grade in school before she left. Back in those days a woman's education was not valued, she was a product of her generation. Nana could not read well enough to read a book and would have difficulty even reading a recipe. Nana never learned to drive either. She said that driving was something she never felt the need to learn to do. She was totally and completely dependent upon her husband for transportation and finances. Nana never had learned to write a check. The story goes that after an oil delivery to her home, the man showed up at the door and told Nana what he was owed. Nana was told that he needed payment and that she could just write him a check. Being a subservient woman, she would always do what she was told, so she went about writing a check. I don't recall the amount for which the check was supposed to be written, but for the sake of example, let's say it was to be a $50.00 check. Later that afternoon, my grandfather received a telephone call from the oil company to tell him that his wife had written a $50,000.00 check for the oil delivery. Needless to say, she knew never to write another check. That was one story she had never lived down, as it had been repeated multiple times over the years. I always remember Nana sitting in her chair at the kitchen table by the window, just looking outside. She seemed content to just sit there for hours and gaze out the window. I never knew what that was about, yet looking back, without her ability to read well, I presume that was her quiet time with God.

Papa was a quiet man. He was a hard worker and had provided for his family through the great depression. As I had mentioned in an earlier chapter, he provided for his family by living off the land. They had fresh vegetables from the garden and their own meat from chicken and pigs. Fresh eggs were obtained daily from the chickens and fresh milk from the cow. He often spoke about barely knowing there had been a depression, since their lives were so self-sufficient. Papa was also a great hunter.

It was common for him to provide fresh game for a meal, as meat variety was a way of life in his home. Deer, squirrel, and rabbit were just a sampling of the menu served in their home. Papa would bring it home; Nana would clean and prepare it. Watching Nana over the years, I quickly came to realize that the hunting was the easy part.

In those early years of raising his family, Papa was also a well-known trapper in the area. From what I understand, he held the record of red fox trapped in New Jersey. The red fox pelts brought a good value, so he provided well for his family. I remember seeing pictures of my grandfather with massive amounts of red fox pellets hanging around him for the picture. He would even go out to check those traps in the dead of the winter after a blizzard. He would walk on top of the snow wearing show-shoes. I grew up thinking that Papa could do anything, gosh, he could walk on top of the snow!

As a child, I remember my mother having a red fox coat which my grandfather had professionally made for her. The coat hung in the back of her closet in a plastic bag. I never remember her wearing it and she obviously did not provide the care that fur coats require. I would often slip my hand up into the bottom plastic bag to feel the fur of that coat, as it felt so soft and smooth. At some point that fox coat disappeared from her closet and I realized that she must have thrown it away. How sad that she did not value that special gift from her father. How sad he must have felt to give her a gift and never see her wear it. I vowed as a young child to always show appreciation for any gift I was given, and to even wear the gift even if I didn't like it. I even recall asking God to make me that type of person, to always appreciate gifts that

I was given and to always appreciate the small things.

Papa was a versatile man. He could make and fix just about anything. As children, we would always take things to Papa to fix. He could always fix it. He could take an old dented up car and rivet in new metal, sand it down and paint it like new. This was not something that he was taught from someone else as a trade, but something he just learned on his own. There was nothing he would not tackle in life. He was an amazing man and I miss him terribly. Papa's ability to fix anything landed him a job at a local summer camp for children. It was not just any summer camp; it was a Jewish-only summer camp. The camp would bus Jewish children in from New York City for a week in the country. The children lived in rustic cabins on wooden cots with a counselor in each cabin. The camp had a beautiful clear lake with all the activities a lake could provide, such as swimming, canoeing, and row boats. There was a raft out in the water and the beach was maintained with beautiful white sand. Activities also included tennis and basketball courts. The camp was way back in the woods on a dirt road which was about 2-3 miles from the main road. It was a huge camp, so there was a lot for Papa to keep up with. Since it was a Jewish camp, the owners were therefore Jewish as well. Papa would complain constantly about his bosses at the camp and call them "cheap." His years working at that camp hardened his heart for the Jewish people, oddly enough, during the same time, my heart was growing for the Jewish people. Our home was on the main road just above the camp entrance. The children from the camp would take daily hikes which would always come up past our home. It would be different children every day, as the hike schedule was divided out, that each group would have one hike during their week at camp. By the time they reached my house, it was time for them to take their lunch break. The counselors leading the group always knew where to stop. This was my favorite activity during my summer break from school, as I would eat lunch with my new Jewish friends. They would pack sandwiches which were usually peanut butter on rye bread, and they would always have one for me too. They always loved the taste of fresh cold well water, so I would bring out pitchers of water and cups, and they would enjoy drinking water without chlorine added. Living in the country, it was hard for me to understand why they loved that water so much, yet living in the city the water was all treated with chlorine. We would talk about everything. We were just kids and we had so much in common, I never realized that there was so much we had that was not in common. As children we never spoke of our differences.

Papa would always refer to his bosses as "mockies." I never understood that word and frankly, I never asked him about that word. I just knew by the tone of voice that he used, that it was a bad word and he was calling the Jewish people... my friends.... that bad name. Later, after I was grown and in a personal relationship with Jesus, I asked God what that word was all about and why Papa had called the Jewish people by that name. God revealed to me that Papa was referring to the Jewish people "mocking" of Jesus. I remember thinking, how could he be so judgmental of the Jews, when he himself did not accept Jesus as his personal savior. Was he any different in his rejection of Jesus? Yet, sadly, he did not realize the condition of his own soul.

As a child I never remember Papa talking about God and he never went to church. He and Nana were married by a justice of the peace, so the opportunity to be in a church, didn't even happen then. The first time I recall Papa being in church was for my brother's wedding in 1978 and then my wedding in 1979. To him, it was obviously just another building and he was merely there to attend a wedding. There was no sense of conviction for being in a church. Without a relationship with Jesus Christ, the church is merely another building.

Upon receiving Jesus as my personal savior as an adult in 1984, I realized the need to witness to my family. They needed to know what Jesus had done for them and they needed to have a personal relationship with the Lord. The first time I spoke with Papa about Jesus, he was quick to remind me that Jesus had indeed been a Jew! Yes Papa, Jesus had been a Jew!

Shouldn't that tell you something? If God chose to send his one and only son to live on this earth as a Jew, should that tell us something? The conversation we had that day was only the first seed planted. It was the first time that I truly saw my grandfather's hardened heart. Yet, I was persistent. I would always tell him, when I left his presence that "I love you and Jesus does too." Years went by, and the persistence remained. There were times when I thought, it would never happen. Papa was getting well up in age and I could see no flicker of hope for a transformation.

On December 16, 1993, Nana went home to be with the Lord. Nana's last years had been very difficult. She had developed Alzheimer's disease and did not remember that Papa was her husband. She would awaken in the night, see the "old" man in bed beside her and become terrified. Thinking she was only a child, she would leave the house, trying to make her way home. After this happened multiple times and my mother got calls from neighbors during the night, concerned that Nana was walking the road, they made the only safe yet difficult decision to place her into a nursing home. Nana had lived her last year in a nursing home. I'm sure those last few years were very difficult for Papa. I can only imagine how he must have felt, seeing his wife's mind slowly slipping away.

Ten years had gone by since I had first started witnessing to Papa, it was now 1994. There had been no change for Papa, and Fred and I had been living in Tennessee for two years. We were no longer just around the corner and able to see him frequently. We were now 800 miles away. Yet, still I prayed that Papa would receive Jesus as his personal Savior. That Christmas, Fred and I bought Papa a Bible. It was a King James Version, red letter edition in giant print with a dark blue leather cover. Inside the front cover, I wrote: "May daily reading bring you closer to receiving Jesus as your personal Savior. We will be praying! With all our love, Fred and Cookie." This was dated December 25, 1994. We traveled to New Jersey for Christmas and I gave it to Papa with a big hug. Papa unwrapped the gift and never removed the Bible from it's box that day.

On July 10, 1995 I mailed a letter to Papa. The letter gave him some Bible verses to read which outlined the crucifixion, the burial, and the resurrection of Jesus, as well as other verses that I had felt compelled to write. Also in that letter, I wrote, "Jesus died on the cross for our sins. Before that time they needed to live by the law, since Jesus died on the cross for our sins, we no longer need to live by the laws. We are in the days of Grace. But we need to ask Jesus to come into our hearts. We have to admit that we are sinners. Fred and I have both been saved. We said the sinner's prayer and asked Jesus to come into our hearts. We know we will go to heaven... the Bible promises that." I then listed Bible verses to support it. The letter went out and no word came back. I continued to pray for Papa to receive Jesus as his personal Savior.

I had made multiple telephone calls to Papa over the years, to just chat and see how he was doing in general. During our conversations, I would never press him about his salvation or ask him if he was reading the Bible. I just wanted him to feel my love without judgment. When ever I ended our conversation, I would always say, "I love you and Jesus does too." This went on year, after year, after year. Still, I continued to pray for his salvation, knowing that God was going to answer my prayers.

In July of 1998, Jessica and I were planning a trip to New Jersey to visit our relatives. Our visits to the north had become few and far between. Fred and David chose not to come this time. Papa was now 89 years old, I knew that this may be the last opportunity to witness to Papa, as he was now living in a nursing home and his health was starting to fail. The week before going to New Jersey, I had prayed with Debbie that Papa would receive Jesus as his personal savior. This was getting to be an old prayer, and frankly, I started wondering if he was ever going to come around. As I was praying with Debbie, I felt compelled to pray "God, please don't let Papa take his last breath until he receives You has his personal savior." Afterward, Debbie and I laughed, that God would be faithful to answer that prayer, yet Papa may need to live to be 130 years old, at this rate, since he was so stubborn.

Jessica, my mom and I visited Papa in the nursing home on July 20, 1998. Papa was resting in bed when we arrived and made no attempt to get out of bed for our visit. I knew that he must be feeling bad, not to get up into the chair. We visited for about an hour, trying to keep the tone light and cheery. I knew that when Mom and Jessica left, I would need to spend some time alone with Papa and witness again. I waited for Mom to start her usual, "It's time to go" speech, and then I walked with Mom and Jessica to the door of Papa's room. I told them I would meet them out in the lobby shortly. Papa's roommate was out of the room and Papa was alone with me. I gently closed the door for privacy, and I could feel my knees shaking as I turned around. In my thoughts, I was saying "Jesus, give me the words today." As I walked toward Papa, I said, "I want to talk to you about Jesus."

Papa started crying like a baby. He started sobbing so loudly, I was concerned that he may be in pain or that something was seriously wrong with him. Kneeling down next to him at the bedside, I looked into Papa's sobbing eyes, and asked "Papa, what is wrong? Are you OK?" Between sobs, Papa said, "I've thought about Jesus all week." My heart was racing now! He had been thinking about Jesus? All week? I put my hand on his arm and asked him if he would like me to lead him in saying the sinner's prayer to accept Jesus as his personal savior? Papa looked at me and said the sweetest word I have ever heard come out of his mouth. He simply said, "Yes," with the biggest smile on his face. YES, he said YES! He wanted to say the sinner's prayer! Years and years of praying and here I was. God was allowing ME the privilege to lead my grandfather in saying the sinner's prayer. Does it get any better then this? I wish

I could say that I eloquently said the sinner's prayer and he calmly repeated it after me. I started sobbing so loud, that I couldn't speak. Not only was Papa going to receive Jesus as his personal savior, but God was giving me the privilege of leading him in the prayer. I felt so humbled that the tears just wouldn't stop. I must have cried for 5 minutes straight before I could compose myself. Papa just held my hand and waited for me to stop crying. He had waited 89 years, what would another 5 minutes mean? After I calmed myself and wiped the tears from my face, I looked at Papa and said, "Now, you know that Jesus was a Jew, right?" He smiled again and said, "Yes, Jesus was a Jew. Isn't that just like God to send a Jew to save me?"

I lead Papa in the sinner's prayer. As I said the words and I waited for him to repeat them, I was in awe of his sincerity. He was saying each word from his heart with such deep meaning.

It had taken him all these years, but he was saying these words from the depths of his soul. As I left his room, that day, I reminded him that we would be back to visit him in March for his 90th Birthday. He was excited that the whole family would be coming for his Birthday, and he was looking forward to seeing Fred and David too. March 26th was his birthday, so we would be returning to see him in just 8 months. When you are 89 years old, arranging a visit which is 8 months away, cannot be a date certain. As I was leaving the room, he said, "If I can't wait until then, I'll see you in heaven." I smiled back and said, "OK Papa, I'll see you either way!" On the way back to Tennessee, I quietly prayed, "Jesus, please let him live for his 90th birthday, so our family can come visit him one more time. Let David and Jessica see Papa since he's been saved"

On March 26, 1999 we arrived at the nursing home to visit with Papa for his 90th birthday. He was sitting up in his wheelchair in the lobby when we arrived. He said that he want to surprise us by personally greeting us at the front door upon our arrival. Yes, that was a surprise. He was more energetic then he had been in years. David was 17 years old now and Jessica was 14. When David and Jessica first saw Papa in the nursing home, they both said, "look at his eyes Mama, look at his eyes." Yes, his eyes surely looked different. Papa had always had blue eyes, but now they were the most beautiful blue we had ever seen. His eyes were clear and sparkling. Yes, his eyes were indeed very different. Jessica said, "You can see Jesus in his eyes. That's the difference." Indeed, the difference was Jesus. The transformation in the last 8 months was amazing. It was a wonderful Birthday celebration and what was to be his last birthday celebrated on earth. God had answered my prayer that he would live for his 90th birthday.

Papa went to be with the Lord on May 18, 1999. Ten months after receiving Jesus as his personal savior and less then two months after his 90th birthday celebration. God had answered my prayer that he wouldn't take his last breath until he had received Jesus as his personal savior. Papa had really cut it close! During this time in my life, I was really questioning God, why He would allow Papa to wait so long. Why had He not drawn Papa to become saved earlier in life, so he could have made an impact on the Kingdom? Yes, he was saved, and I knew I would see him in heaven, but he never had the opportunity to let his light shine. I knew that God was in control, and I just wanted to see this through God's eyes to better understand it. God was silent. There was no still small voice.

There was no answer coming, so I thought, *it's not mine to know.*

My mom and I had to go to the nursing home to retrieve Papa's personal items. We waited until the day after the funeral and drove to the nursing home to complete the dreaded task. Alone in his room, we gathered his items and placed them into the boxes we had brought with us. I remember thinking; I didn't know why we had come, that there was nothing worth keeping. It was stuff that I would have just thrown away. Then, I opened the top drawer of his bedside table and saw the Bible. It was the Bible that Fred and I had given to Papa on December 25, 1994. He had kept it in the original box, and as I opened the Bible, I was surprised to see there were papers stuck in among the pages. The first papers I saw were folded up and placed in the front of the Bible. It was the letter that I had mailed to Papa in

1995. It was the letter with Bible verses, where I had written about the sinner's prayer. As I flipped through the Bible, I quickly realized that there were papers placed in each section of the Bible, where the verses were, that I had listed in that letter. He had taken the time to look up and read each Bible verse I had included in the letter. Slipped in the Bible between the book of Romans and 1st Corinthians was an envelope. As I picked up the envelope, I saw that it was the envelope in which I had mailed the Bible verses to Papa. It was post marked July 10, 1995 and the post mark was smeared with water. As I looked at the envelope, God revealed that was not a smear from water, but smears form Papa's tears. That Papa had cried while holding the envelope. In First John was the last page of my letter. It was placed next to the verse First John 1: 9 from the letter. On the last page of the letter, I had written, "I pray that you will make the decision to ask Jesus into your heart. By making the decision to accept Jesus as your personal savior would mean that you and I would be together forever in eternity. It would mean so much to me to know that you will be there too. The prayer is easy; 'Jesus, I admit that I am a sinner. I know that you died on the cross for my sins. Please come into my heart and save me.' Jesus loves you and so do I. Love Cookie." I smiled as I read this last page, since I had signed the letter with the name he had called me as a child and had continued to call me into adulthood. I had told him so many times, that I didn't want him to call me that any more, yet here in this letter, I had signed the letter using the name that he had held onto tightly over the years. I sat there on the bed in the nursing home, wondering, if that was what made him cry on the envelope. I have his Bible now. It is a priceless reminder, that continued prayers, said without ceasing, will be answered. Praise God.

As my mom and I were leaving the nursing home that afternoon, for the last time, we were stopped at the nurse's station by a nursing assistant, who obviously wanted to talk. She said she was sad to have lost "Allen," and that she will "always remember him." I thanked her for her kind words and started to walk away, when she reached out and touched my arm. Then she said, "Your grandfather changed this place in the last few months, you know. After he received Jesus as his personal savior, it was his mission to tell everybody here." I turned to her, and said, "Really?" She said, "Oh, yes! He was a changed man. We couldn't keep him in that bed after that day. Before that day, we always had a hard time convincing him to get out of bed. After that day, we used to have to beg him to go to bed at night, so he could rest.

He went room to room witnessing to everybody who lived here. He told everyone how much Jesus loved them and that Jesus had died on the cross for their sins. He was nice about it. Nobody ever complained. He told everybody how he had wasted his life without Jesus." I was totally stunned by what this nursing assistant was telling me. Then, she went on, "Oh yes, he even had certain Bible verses marked in his Bible that he would love to share. He would sit by the front door and tell people as they came and went that Jesus loved them." She laughed, and then added, "He may have gotten a late start, but he sure was a preacher here." I hugged that precious nursing assistant and walked out of that nursing home with a new perspective. Thank you God for the lesson that day, the affect a 90 year old man had made on an entire nursing home. He had less than a year to live after he had accepted Jesus as his personal savior, yet he witnessed far more that most Christians do in their entire lifetime. It's hard to know how many people he may have lead to the Lord during those eight months. It's amazing!

It doesn't mater how old you are when you receive Jesus as your personal savior. God can use you wherever you are and regardless of how old you are.

Reflecting on the salvation dates for my Papa and both my children; David and Jessica, it is amazing that they were all three saved on the same month and day just 5 years apart. They all three accepted Jesus as their personal savior on July 20th. That is surely no coincidence. Absolutely not! God is showing his love for this family and his faithfulness.

Praise God! 'Use me Lord.' To God be all the Glory!

1 John 1:9

"If we confess our sins, He is faithful and just and will forgive us our sins and purify us from all unrighteousness."

Chapter 14

I think the Holy Spirit likes mustard

✝

Growing in the spirit makes you thirsty for more knowledge. We were now attending a spirit-filled church, yet I wanted to know more. We were attending a small church home group weekly, in addition to church services. The small home-group allowed for more personal questions and also developed friendships that have remained precious. The small home group allowed for prayers and the laying-on of hands for healing in a small non-threatening friendly environment.

During one evening at the home group, one of the men had complained of back and neck pain. I shared with the group that God had given me the gift of healing, although I had only used it twice. I told them about my hands getting red and hot during church services, yet I had not felt comfortable or confident enough to go and lay hands on anyone in church. That evening, I stood behind that man at home group and placed my hands on the back of his neck and prayed for his healing. The heat in my hands exploded as I touched him. Not only did the heat increase, but I could feel it releasing into the man. Along with the heat sensation was also a surge of power. This power, which I knew to be the Holy Spirit, caused my hands to vibrate. As I looked at my hands, the vibration was not visible, yet felt.

He was healed! He told me that his back and neck pain were gone. Praise God. We then had a very important discussion in the home group, about always giving Praise and the credit to God. It was a gift for us to use to bless others, yet, never to take the praise for the healing, but to pass it on to God! Always! This was a valuable teaching, as it would have been easy, in the flesh, to say, "Look what I did." From that first healing months earlier and since, the praise has always been redirected to God immediately.

I remained thirsty for more knowledge. I am grateful that God has kept me thirsty for more and never complacent in what I had already experienced. While watching television one day, I had come upon the Benny Hinn Ministry show. Benny Hinn was an evangelist with the gift of healing. I watched for several months and became a partner. Fred and I had attended a miracle crusade. I was so amazed that the healings had occurred by the Holy Spirit and without one touch from Benny Hinn himself, in most cases. Benny Hinn was a humble willing vessel. The small parts shown on TV of the Benny Hinn Miracle Crusades didn't fully show that miracles happened prior to his arrival onto the stage. Benny Hinn was always reflecting the glory for the miracles back to the Holy Spirit and never taking any credit himself for the miracles. The environment of faith pleased the Holy Spirit, the result being miracles displayed. I soon realized there was a partner convention coming within driving distance to our house. When I discussed this partner convention with Fred, I could not see any excitement in attending. So, I prayed... "God, if we are supposed to attend, please tell Fred."

Within a few days, Fred was encouraging me to get tickets to attend the partner convention. I got tickets for our family of 4 to attend. David and Jessica had also been watching the

Benny Hinn shows with me in the evening. I would tape the shows during the day while I was working, so we could watch them in the evening. The kids were also excited about going to the partner convention.

The partner convention was amazing. Pastor Benny Hinn had several teaching sessions throughout the two day convention. We were learning what we knew we had been thirsty for. Watching Pastor Hinn revealed his heart for the lost and his desire to share his knowledge. This was not just a man doing a job! Benny Hinn was living the true Christian life. On the last day of the partner convention, all the partners were encouraged to come forward, so Pastor Hinn could personally lay hands on and pray blessing on each one. This process took hours, as there were so many people there. I knew it would be worth the wait, as I waited my turn. At his touch, people were falling out in the spirit.

To some, he was speaking and to others, he was just giving a touch and moving on.

As it came my turn, I was hoping to hear what he would say to my husband and children, but since I was in line before them, that opportunity did not happen. As Pastor Hinn gently touched my forehead, he looked into my eyes and said, "God is using you mightily. You haven't seen anything yet."

The next thing I remember, I was driving. I do not remember returning to my seat to gather my personal items, although my family assures me that I did. I do not remember walking nearly the mile to the car, which my family assures me that I did, and yet... I was driving! Obviously I had been in the spirit for... an hour? Fred said I had been driving for an hour already. I had driven through Atlanta, Georgia down town traffic and was on the interstate.

Fred said I had also eaten. I had eaten what? Fred told me that on the way out of the convention, there were brown bags for each partner leaving the convention as an evening snack. I had chosen and eaten a roast beef sandwich with mustard. Mustard? I ate mustard? I would *never* eat mustard on my roast beef. I would only have eaten mayonnaise on roast beef. I was sure he was teasing me now! David and Jessica assured me that I had personally chosen the roast beef with mustard myself, although there were roast beef sandwiches available with mayonnaise, and had consumed the entire sandwich. They also said I had not spoken as I drove, but had been humming the sweetest sound.

I'm sure something huge happened that night. When Pastor Hinn touched me, I entered into a new realm as the Holy Spirit did a good work. God had used Pastor Hinn and as I entered a new level, God had allowed me to function physically while the Holy Spirit remained at work.

Amazing! God is truly amazing! Praise God. To God be all the Glory!

1 Corinthians 2:9

However, as it is written: "No eye has seen, no ear has heard, no mind has conceived what God has prepared for those who love him."

Chapter 15

God turned the tornado

✝

Vacations are a very important part of life. I was raised to understand that a yearly vacation is important for the family, as it allows time to relax, have some fun together, and relate in a different environment. Our lives are packed full of distractions and business which sometimes causes us to entirely retreat from family communication. We may all be in the same house, yet everyone is busy doing something different which in fact prevents relationship building in the way which God had in mind when He created us in the first place. I've always known that a small home makes for a tighter family, as they cannot really get away from each other so easily. When we moved from a 3,000 square foot house in New Jersey to an 1800 square foot house in Tennessee, I knew that God had a plan. Not only had we down-sized, but we had moved from a real house to a double wide. For years I struggled with that decision to purchase a double wide trailer and would never allow myself to say the word 'trailer.' It sounds silly now, but it was a 'pride' thing. God was growing me in humility and I was dragging my feet. Pride is a really hard thing to break, when you are not submitting to the change. By living in the double wide trailer for seventeen years, I learned that you can't judge a book by its cover. I had also come to realize that by living in that double wide trailer I was on a level playing field with many of the people I would be leading to the Lord. God always has a plan, and I am thankful that I do not get a sneak-peak prior to stepping out in obedience. Had I known his entire plan prior to stepping out in obedience, I may not have been so easily lead. It's easier to be lead, when only seeing one very short section of the path. Looking back now, I would not have changed one thing.

Over the years we have taken many nice vacations. We have always involved the children when planning the vacation location being sure to include educational stops along the way. There are many places to visit in the United States which have little or no cost. We have always tried to instill the value into our children, that the most expensive is not always the best experience. When we lived in New Jersey, our vacations would often take us to the south. Going to a warm beach in the middle of a brutal winter and returning with a tan, was always a nice experience. The children grew up realizing that a piece of bologna placed between two slices of bread was an adequate meal and would allow that extra saved money to be used for seeing attractions along the way. During one vacation to the south we stopped at the Coke exhibit in Atlanta, Georgia. I smile now, thinking about how Fred and the children reacted when I suggested stopping there along the way. I remember the children saying that they would do it 'for you Mom,' fully not expecting to have any enjoyment there. To their amazement they enjoyed the 'Coke' attraction and are still talking about all the different favors of Coke from around the world that they sampled. On one vacation we stopped at a museum that actually permitted the children to 'feel' how it felt to be handicapped. I can't even remember where that museum was, but the impact on the children was lasting. They experienced how it felt to be in a wheelchair. They actually had to push the wheelchair themselves through different ground cover such as dirt, gravel, and grass. The experience included using crutches, arm braces and leg braces as well as the experience of being blind. The children gained a tremendous insight that day for the handicapped. I thank God for every experience and His obvious guidance and direction in our vacation plans. We were always 'amazed' what we came upon during our travel, yet God knew exactly what was needed during each moment in our lives.

One memorable vacation took us to the Grand Canyon. We had decided that we would drive from Tennessee to the Grand Canyon so we could see and experience the journey along the way. We drove the southern route out to the Grand Canyon and saw our first oil drilling rig in Texas. When we saw the first oil drilling rig along the highway we stopped along the edge of the road to take a picture, since we had never seen one of those before. There was a fence along the edge of the road, so it was a struggle to get a good picture of that oil drilling rig. We laughed as we drove along, since we later saw thousands of oil drilling rigs.

Along the way, my son was amazed at the tumble weeds rolling across the desert on both sides of the road. We had driven for many miles with his watching those tumble weeds, when he asked if he could have one. I had always tried to raise the children with positive affirmation instead of always just saying 'no.' Therefore, my response to this 'silly' request for a tumble weed, was "Yes, if the tumble weed runs right into our car, we will stop and pick it up for you." Now, what would be the chance that a tumble weed would roll across the desert and smack into our car? I felt that was a safe way of saying 'no' to him. We drove along enjoying the scenery and the beautiful sunshine that was streaming into the car. I was amazed at how flat the land was as we were driving. The eastern part of the country is full of mountains and hills, yet out here in the west, it was flat. It was amazingly flat. So flat, in fact... that a tumble weed rolled right across that desert and smacked into the front of our car. "Yes, son, it's yours," I laughed, as I stopped the car. We had just enough room in the car trunk for that tumble weed. It was the perfect size to fit. Our son was delighted and thanked God for answering his prayer for that tumble weed! The tumble weed had rolled smack into our car, because our son had prayed for one. Isn't it just like God to gift His children? God wants his children to have the desires of our hearts.

It was a delightful trip to the Grand Canyon and upon arriving at the edge of the Canyon; we were in total awe of God's creation. The Grand Canyon was huge! It was deeper and wider then I had expected and the layers of rock had the most vibrant colors. I had seen many pictures and movies on television of the Grand Canyon, yet nothing could be more beautiful the seeing it through your own eyes. We spend many hours looking from different locations along the Grand Canyon's rim. It was a trip of a lifetime and one that was not forgotten.

The return trip home was taken by the northern route. We drove up into Colorado and drove up Pike's Peak. I drove the entire way up the mountain, which continually circled around and around and around to get to the top. The road was dirt and most edges along the way were shear cliff drop-offs without any guard-rails for protection. On top of the mountain, the air was thin and made you feel slow and light-headed. Again, this was an adventure; Fred had the 'privilege' of driving back down that mountain.

As we traveled through Kansas we all wondered if we would see a tornado along the way. The weather looked OK, yet the forecast had mentioned a chance of bad weather and thunder storms. The children we thinking it would be 'awesome' to see a tornado, yet I was praying there would be no tornado any where near where we were traveling. We were driving through "Tornado Alley" and that was as close as I wanted to be to an actual tornado. We never did see a tornado as we were driving through tornado alley, for which I was most grateful.

We arrived back in Tennessee after our two-week vacation excited for all we had seen and exhausted for trying to see everything along the way. I knew that we would probably never make a trip back there again by car, so we had agreed to see as much as possible. We had seen everything and although vacations are great, it is always a comforting feeling arriving back in your own town. As we drove back into our home area, we were excited about getting back home and sleeping in our own beds that night. There is nothing like your own bed and your own pillow, after being away for two weeks. As we started to turn onto our road we stopped the car and gazed in horror at the path of destruction which lay ahead of us. It was obvious that the path had been a tornado, as the path cut through the tree line directly across from the entrance to our road. As we turned and started driving up our road, the path of destruction ran parallel to the road on the left side. The tornado had barely missed the first two houses on the road, yet their sheds and porches were scattered all over their property. As we continued to travel the short distance to our home, we knew this tornado had been headed straight for our house. We let out sighs of relief to see our home still standing. It was amazing. The tornado had been headed directly for our house and then stopped? Where did it go and where did it turn? It didn't make any sense. As we pulled the car into the driveway and looked down the road, the path of the tornado was headed directly for our house. The path had come to our property line and made a 90-degree turn. Why would a tornado make a 90-degree turn? There is no physical reason. This was amazing.

As I stood there in our driveway looking at the path the tornado had taken, God reminded me of the day I had prayed over our property. Not long after moving to Tennessee, I had felt lead by God to pray over the property. I felt instructed to pray along the property lines and dedicate the property to his glory. I had walked the entire 23 acres and proclaimed the property lines would be protected for our family's safety that no evil may enter in ever. God had prompted me to pray along the property lines and years later the tornado could not pass into our property. I stood there crying over God's protection and His direction that day several years prior, to pray over our property. My husband Fred rode the 4-wheeler out the property line to see where the tornado path had gone. When he returned, he shared that the tornado had cut a path along our property line and knocked down several very large trees along the edge of our property yet never crossing onto our property along the way.

I am amazed and in awe of God's constant provision and unfailing protection. When we are obedient to do what the Lord is asking us to do, we cannot always see the outcome and results. Often prayers are said; years later the outcome is still not revealed to us. We must be obedient and know that God's plans are not always for us to see the results. When we pray for others, we are to pray and let it go. Yet, sometimes, God allows us the privilege to see results. For those times, I am most thankful. It pushes us onward in faith, knowing that God has his eye on the prize.

Praise God! To God be all the Glory!

Matthew 17:20

He replied, "Because you have so little faith, I tell you the truth, if you have faith as small as a mustard seed, you can say to this mountain, 'move from here to there' and it will move, Nothing will be impossible for you."

Chapter 16

He's having a Seizure

✝

When I first became a nurse I worked in the fast-paced hospital setting. I gained years of experience working in various settings such as medical, surgical, pediatrics, emergency room and the Intensive care unit. The environment was always changing. One would never know from moment to moment what may be required. I loved the fast pace and felt I was really making a difference. I laugh when I think about 'making a difference.' When people apply to nursing school, they always say they 'want to make a difference,' much like when a young woman enters a beauty pageant, she will say she wants 'world peace.' It's those common traits and longings that draw us together in the nursing profession. We all just want to 'make a difference.' In doing so, nurses work long hours and stay when the next nurse scheduled to work becomes ill and can't come to work. It's a profession where hearts lead the way.

When I was still living and working in New Jersey, I saw an ad in the local news paper for a position at a local nursing home. I had never worked in a nursing home before, as I had worked my entire career at that point at the same hospital. I had never thought about working in a nursing home, since I had always heard about the bad reputations and poor care given to the elderly. The advertisement for this job really intrigued me. The position being advertised was for a Director of Staff education.

I loved to train people; I had trained many new nurses at the hospital and I thought, this may be a good job for me. I submitted my resume to the nursing home and was called for an interview within a few days. I was excited about having a position where I could train the staff, and looked forward to the interview. When I walked into the nursing home that afternoon for my interview, the stench almost knocked me over. I had never in my life smelled anything that bad. The smell was so intense in fact, that I felt myself wanting to gag as I sat in the lobby. I almost got up and left without interviewing, but for some crazy idea, I thought that once I entered through the next set of doors, the smell would be gone. What was I thinking? Obviously, I had never been in a nursing home before, so I had no idea what to expect. When the lady came and escorted me back to be interviewed, she took me through the next set of doors. The odor got worse. It was unbelievable. I knew that I could never work in a place that smelled this bad. The odor was not as apparent in the office I was being interviewed in, yet I knew that I could not work there. After the interview was completed, I was offered the job. I was pleased to be offered the job, as it made me feel valuable, yet as we talked about the salary for the position, I announced that my expectations for the position would require twice the pay that they were offering. I remember thinking, that if I would have to work in those conditions, they would have to pay me dearly. I did not get that job and I left there feeling so sad that the elderly population had to exist in that environment. I prayed that God would bring the right people to work in nursing homes, who would change it. The elderly deserved to have great care and should not need to live in an environment that smelled so badly.

After moving to Tennessee and getting my first job in a nursing home as a Director of Nursing, I realized that God had been drawing me to work with the elderly. I knew that I would be required to *make the difference* that I had prayed years earlier. I worked long hours and worked side-by-side with the staff to show them the right way. When you are working in a facility for hours each day, you sometimes become desensitized to odors. I would have my husband and children visit the facility weekly, to be sure there were no smells that I was missing. I had suddenly realized my passion for caring for the elderly and my *assignment* to make the difference, which I had prayed for earlier in my career. Over the years, I had several jobs working for nursing home companies and helping care for the elderly residents. The days of expecting nursing homes to smell bad are gone. Most nursing homes now take pride in great care provided and no lingering odors throughout the facility. Striving for a home-like environment and more strict state and federal regulations have made a huge difference in the lives of our elderly population living in nursing homes.

As I was working in one nursing home as a supervisor, I was often called 'stat' over-head on the paging system to a location where a nurse or resident needed immediate assistance. The word 'stat' meant it was an emergency and the response needed to be instant. The call for 'stat' assistance would mean running to that location without advance knowledge of what you may need to contend with upon your arrival. It often meant that someone had stopped breathing, so you would get mentally prepared during your run to the location for possibility having to perform CPR.

As a Christian, I had always tried to be the same person when I was at work or at home. I wanted my testimony to be evident in everything I said and did. Unfortunately I did not always show my best side. When I was frustrated or feeling over worked, I would have to apologize later and ask for forgiveness. Christians are not perfect, yet since we are always being watched for our commitment, we need to be especially careful to let our light shine. While at work there are many things you cannot do as a Christian, if you want to keep your job. For example: It is never acceptable to preach your faith in the front lobby to visitors arriving or cast out demons in the parking lot. You must realize that I am choosing areas which may be considered extreme for the purpose of this illustration, yet while working a job, any praying may need to be done in quiet or in a non-public area. I would often pray for residents and staff, yet it was always at their request and surely behind a closed door. I wanted God to 'Use Me' and also knew I needed to be politically correct to please the company for which I was working.

One afternoon I was paged 'stat' on the over-head paging system to the opposite end of the facility. I took off running, knowing that someone's life was hanging in the balance and I needed to get there immediately. As I came running down through the center of the nursing home, I could see straight into the unit I had been called to. Sitting in the hall was a resident in his wheelchair having a grand-mal seizure. He was having such a violent seizure that no one could get close enough to him to offer any protection. He was sitting with his back against the wall and was banging his head violently against the wall as his arms flailed wildly keeping the staff at a distance. A crowd had gathered around him including the Administrator of the facility, yet no one could get close enough to provide any assistance to this poor man.

Somewhere along the way, as I was running, I forgot where I was. I had forgotten that I was a nurse at work in this nursing home, strange as that may sound. When I arrived at the location where the man was continuing to have a grand-mal seizure, I abruptly and boldly put my hand on the side of his head barely coming to a stop, and with all authority and in a loud voice proclaimed, "I rebuke you in the name of Jesus!" The man's seizure immediately stopped, his eyes opened and he looked directly at me, totally alert and responsive, and said, "What happened?" For anyone who has ever seen a seizure, you know that after a seizure, the person is very lethargic and tired. They do not open their eyes wide nor do they even look alert. For all intensive purposes, after a seizure, people act dopey and seldom even are able to speak. By now, I was realizing what I had just done. I was realizing that there was a crowd of people gathered around including the Administrator of the facility. All eyes were now on me. I wasn't exactly sure what I should say or do at that point. I wasn't sure how anyone would react to what had just happened and surely knew this was not the time or place to discuss the power of God. All I could think to say was, "There ya go. It's done. Thank you Jesus," as I walked away.

The Administrator never did discuss that event with me. There were many conversations behind closed doors about the power of God, as God used that event to open eyes. Many residents got saved in that facility in the coming weeks, as a new boldness came over the Christians who worked there. I often think back and laugh about that day. Seeing a professional nurse run down the hall to rebuke the devil, I'm sure was a first for all the people standing there. I smile when I think back to saying, "There ya go. It's done. Thank you Jesus"

Use me Lord! Praise God... Use me! Let your will be done.

Mark 9:25
When Jesus saw that a crowd was running to the scene, He rebuked the evil spirit, "You deaf and mute spirit, He said, "I command you, come out of him and never enter him again."

Proverbs 30:5
Every word of God is flawless; He is a shield to those who take refuge in him.

Chapter 17

Watching a miracle on the monitor

✝

The morning of September 1, 2000 I was driving to work and as usual, I was praying that God would 'Use Me' today. It was a beautiful day and as I drove along, I praised the Lord for everything I could think of to praise him for His blessings to me. I thanked God for my job, for my car, for my family, and for the gifts He was giving me in the Spirit and allowing me the privilege to glorify his name. As I continued to pray for God to Use Me that day, I felt the Lord say 'mightily.' "Yes Lord," I prayed, "Lord

Use Me Mightily today, in the name of Jesus."
I knew in my spirit that this was going to be a
glorious day. I couldn't wait to see what God's
plans were for me today. I arrived at work and
it really felt like any other day. There were no
bells and whistles to alert me to any up coming
event. I was busy performing my regular nursing
duties for the elderly residents God had put in
my care. Suddenly a nurse from another unit
came running to get me. She had run from
the other end of the facility and I immediately
wondered why she had run all that way, when
she could have paged me 'stat' on the over-
head paging system. As she tried to catch her
breath and speak, I suddenly realized that this
was an emergency spiritual need. Before she
was even able to speak one word, the Holy
Spirit told me that I needed to pray healing for
a resident. When she was able to catch her
breath and speak, the nurse told me that she

had chosen to run and get me, not page over-head because she wanted me to come and pray for a resident's healing. She told me that if she had paged over-head for me to come to her assistance, other nurses would also come, knowing that it was an emergency. The decision of what to do for the resident would then become medical treatment focused instead of prayer focused. As we ran all the way back to the unit she was working on, at the other end of the facility, I silently prayed "Use Me Mightily Lord."

As I entered the resident's room, I closed the door behind me to allow privacy for what was about to happen. The privacy was not only for the resident but also for me. I knew praying was not the acceptable means of medical intervention and realized I could easily get terminated from my job for what I was about to do. It may sound a bit crazy to think someone could get fired from their job for praying, but unfortunately, that is the way it works in the real world. I was surprised to see that the resident was connected to a monitor. Having a monitor connected is not something you would expect to see in a nursing home, yet this resident's condition was so unstable, they had chosen to have the device connected to safety monitor the resident for any sudden changes. As I glanced at the monitor, her heart rate was 114 per minute, her respiratory rate was 32 per minute and her oxygen saturation was at 60%. Yes, her heart was beating a bit too fast and her respiratory rate was a bit too high, yet the oxygen saturation at 60% was way too low. At that rate, she was not getting adequate oxygen to the brain and the condition could only get worse. As I approached the lady laying in the bed, she looked at me with eyes starring wide open in fear as if she knew that she was about to die. I recognized that look as feeling like death was imminent, as I had experienced that same feeling within the last 2 years. Not being able to breathe is a terrible feeling. One that you can only explain if you have lived through it. The nurse that had run the entire length of the facility to get me was now telling the resident, "This is that nurse I told you about, the one that stopped that man's seizure by just touching him. God uses her." I asked the resident if I could pray for her and she said, "Yes." It was very difficult for her to speak and I realized that just saying 'yes,' had been a struggle for her to say. Then I asked her if I could lay my hands on her as I prayed for her healing, and again she said, "Yes." Again she struggled to speak and I could see the look in her eyes begging me not to ask any more questions but to do something. The Holy Spirit had told me years before that I must always ask before touching anyone in prayer. Part of the healing experience is that they must consent to being touched, as that increases their faith by their consenting to allow it to occur. Asking the person first before touching them is polite and respectful as well as providing the slight delay which allows the Holy Spirit to prepare you, in the event that the person has an oppressive spirit attached. I have always found it helpful to pray protection over myself and those around prior to a hand-on healing, in the event that an evil spirit is present. In this particular case, I felt there was something present, which would need to be told to leave, so I quickly prayed protection for myself and everyone in the facility, that any evil spirit which was required to leave could only report to the feet of Jesus.

As I laid my hands gently on the resident's chest, I prayed out loud for her "breathing to come under God's control" and her "heart to come under God's control." I prayed for the "oxygen to increase in the name of Jesus." And "in the Name of Jesus, for any spirit that was not of God to leave now and report to the feet of Jesus." As I was praying, I heard the still small voice of the Holy Spirit say "open your eyes and see." I would always close my eyes during prayer. I had been taught to pray with my eyes closed as a young child in Sunday school and had just always done it. I realized that day, that it's OK to keep your eyes open when you pray or when you speak to God. There is no law saying that you must close your eyes. As I was pondering his words, the Holy Spirit said, "I have never said to close your eyes." What a revelation! As I opened my eyes I first looked at the resident's face. She was gently weeping and her respirations were slower. I looked up at the monitor to see what God was doing. I had only been praying for less then 2 minutes and her heart rate was a normal 72 beats per minute, her respiratory rate was a normal 20 per minute and her oxygen saturation was already up to 90%. Amazing! To see God's healing effect displayed on a monitor was yet another ultimate gift from God. It was the first time I had gotten to see a miracle displayed on a monitor. I said "Amen," then said, "Thank you God for this miracle." I looked at the nurse who had run to get me earlier. The nurse was down on her knees at the other side of the bed from me. The nurse was sobbing loudly with her forehead resting on the edge of the mattress. I looked at the resident, she also was sobbing loudly. I stood there for a moment praising God, allowing the Holy Spirit to complete his work in both the resident and the nurse. Sobbing can be good for the spirit as it is refreshing and the result of the revelation that we are useless without God's intervention.

When the sobbing had stopped, the resident said she hadn't felt that good in years. She said that her breathing had never been that easy for as long as she could remember. She said that she could no longer feel her heart 'pounding' in her chest. She said that it had pounded in her chest for years. Prior to my running to the room that morning, I had not seen this resident, as she had just been admitted to the facility earlier that morning. The resident shared her medical history with me, which included congestive heart failure, emphysema, a congenital heart defect, and pulmonary fibrosis. She shared with me that she had been admitted to the nursing home that morning for comfort measures only, as she was not expected to live much longer. The resident said she was told she would probably have less then a month to live.

Well, I realize that God does not perform a miracle like that if He doesn't have other plans for this sweet soul. I asked her if she had "Jesus in her heart" and she replied, "I've gone to church since I was a young child." Now, that is not the right answer! Going to church does not mean that you have a personal relationship with Jesus, nor does it mean that you have asked Jesus to be your personal savior. At that point I shared with her about how Jesus had died on the cross for her sins. From going to church she already knew all the church stories. It's really easy to lead someone to receive Jesus as their personal savior when they have gone to church all their lives. They know all about the cross and the resurrection. They even know about "having Jesus in their heart." Yet, so many people miss the biggest point. The confession must come out of their mouths. They must say it for themselves. No one else can say the sinner's prayer for them or pray over them. As I shared with this sweet soul, that she needed to say the sinner's prayer and with her own mouth confess Jesus as her personal savior, I could see the 'lights' come on. She had missed that one huge step. In her mind, going to church regularly and listening to the preacher teach the word of God was what was needed. She asked me what the sinner's prayer said. I told her that the sinner's prayer was just confessing that she is a sinner and that Jesus had died on the cross to take the punishment onto Himself for her sins, and then ask Him to forgive her sins and ask Jesus to come into her heart so she can live for Him. She asked me to help her and I reminded her again that the words must come from her mouth, yet I would say the prayer and she could repeat the words. I lead her slowly in the sinner's prayer and she repeated each word after me with conviction. At the end of the prayer, when she had said 'amen,' the nurse who was still on her knees on the other side of the bed started sobbing again. She was sobbing really loud. I thought that she was just overcome with joy that this resident had just received Jesus as her personal savior. Yet, when the nurse stopped crying and was able to speak, she reported that she too had said the sinner's prayer, for the first time, along with us. She said that although she had been in church her entire life, she had never said the sinner's prayer. She recalled as a teenager the preacher asking if anyone wanted to give their lives to God, to come forward, and she had gone forward. Yet, she never said anything. She clearly remembers the preacher praying over those who had come forward. She had never asked Jesus into her heart before. She started sobbing again and saying, "I could have missed it. I could have missed Heaven."

Praise God! That was a 2-for 1 deal. Isn't that just like God, to show up and show off? We did a group hug I joked with them about being neighbors in Heaven, before proclaiming that I really needed to get back to work. As I turned to leave the room I glanced at the monitor one last time. Her heart and respiratory rates were still normal, yet her oxygen saturation level was now at 100%. I spoke out loud to the resident that her oxygen saturation level which was displayed on the monitor, was now at 100%. The resident said that had not been over 90% in the last 10 years. As I opened the door to leave the room, she called out behind me and asked what my name was. She said that she needed to know my name. I never did tell her my name. "Praise God," I said as I left the room, "You give God all the glory for your healing. That wasn't me that healed you. You don't need to know my name. You give God all the Glory. You praise God for your new heart, your new lungs and your new beginning."

The facility was quiet as I walked back through the entire building to my assigned unit. No one had been aware of the glory that had occurred in that resident room. As I walked back to my unit, the LPN was still giving the residents their medications and the nursing assistants were still caring for their residents. A Miracle had just happened and the world was progressing as if nothing had happened. One resident received her complete healing and two people had received Jesus as their personal savior, yet in the short 30 minutes that I had been gone, nothing in this physical world had changed. I remember thinking, "In the blink of an eye. Jesus would come when they least expected it." Then I heard that still small voice of the Holy Spirit saying, "You have much work to do." Yes Lord! Use Me Lord. To God be all the Glory!

The next morning when I arrived at work, I went over to the resident's room to see her. I wanted to check in on her and be sure she had retained her healing. The enemy loves to steal away healings, so I wanted to stop by and check on her. Her bed was empty and the bed was freshly made with clean white linens and a new flowered bedspread. I walked back to the nurse's station and asked the nurse standing at the nurse's station where the resident was. I was told, "Oh, she went home this morning. She felt great and her physician discharged her when we told him the monitor readings. Her oxygen saturation level had stayed at 100% all night and her heart and respirations remained normal. She had been up walking around most of the night, since she felt great. She wanted to go home to play with her grandchildren, since she's never been able to hold them or play with them since she had always been so short of breath." I thanked the nurse then turned to walk away, as I said, "Praise God! I'll have to wait to see her in heaven!"

1 Peter 2:24

He himself bore our sins in his body on the tree, so that we might die to sins and live for righteousness; by his wounds you have been healed.

Chapter 18

Three Crosses in the Sky

✝

While in church one day, a friend came over to me and asked me to pray for her father-in-law. She said that he had never received Jesus as his personal savior and was very ill. She told me that he had a stroke and was unable to speak. The doctors reported his prognosis to be extremely poor and they would be sending him to a nursing home to provide for this physical care needs due to the severity of the stroke.

I prayed with her right there and then. I had come to realize over these past few years, not to just tell someone that I would pray, but to join hands with them right then and pray. God tells us in His word, when two or more are joined in prayer, that He is there in their midst. As we prayed for her father-in-law, I could feel her hopelessness in the situation. This man had already had a stroke, couldn't speak and probably had other serious limitations from the stroke as well. She shared with me that his wife was a wonderful Christian lady and had been praying for his salvation for many years without success. The shock of losing him was bad enough, but to lose him without his having received Jesus as his savior, was devastating. As we prayed, the thought came into my head with that still soft voice…the voice of the Holy Spirit, "Pray that he will not take his last breath until he accepts Me." Wow, OK Lord! I told my friend what I had just heard, and we prayed that prayer. "Lord, please do not allow him to take his last breath until he accepts you as his personal savior." I knew that prayer had worked for my Grandfather, so I was confident it would work now.

The next day at the nursing home, I reviewed the records for a pending admission. This man had the same last name as my friend from church. Reviewing his record, I soon realized this was her father-in-law. I could feel my heart leap in my chest. He would be coming to live in my nursing home today. I could not wait for him to get there. As I helped to prepare his room for his arrival, I prayed over the bed asking for God to "use me" however He wanted to. "Use me Lord," I prayed, "to make a difference in his life and in the lives of his family."

Mr. Irwin arrived late that afternoon to the facility. While assisting him from the stretcher into the facility bed, I was so disappointed in his condition. He was unable to assist with any movement of his own body. The stroke had affected his entire body. His eyes looked blank and dull. When I spoke to him, there was no response. I tried to get some type of response by mentioning that I knew his daughter-in-law and mentioned her and his son by name. There was no response at all. He would look off into space, as if no one was speaking to him. His wife was there with him when he arrived and you could see the torment in her eyes that her husband was dying without Jesus. I held her in my arms and tried to console her. She had such a sweet spirit and was obviously not dealing well with the pending outcome.

When I left to go home that day, I again prayed, "Lord, please don't let him take his last breath until he accepts you as his personal savior." As I spoke with God, I thought that there was no way Mr. Irwin would be able to say the sinner's prayer although maybe he would just make his peace with God before he passed away. That we would never know. As I thought about that, I instantly thought about his wife. She would not have that comfort of knowing that he had accepted Jesus as his personal savior. How sad that would be for her, I thought. Then I prayed, "Lord, please don't let him take his last breath until he accepts you as is personal savior AND give his wife the assurance of knowing he will spend eternity in heaven." Wow, I thought, that is a tall order! God is mighty and I can't wait to see how He's going to pull this one off!

God awoke me at 3 AM the next morning. Waking in the middle of the night had become a common event for me over the last few years. God would place someone on my heart, I would pray while in bed, and then roll back over and return to sleep. This was different, as I was told to get up out of the bed. As I got up from the bed, I grabbed by Bible from the night table, assuming this would be a larger scale prayer event. Going into the living room, trying to be quiet, so the family would not get awakened, I sat down on the couch. That still quiet little voice of the Holy Spirit told me, "Pray for Mr. Irwin. Pray that his mind would be restored for understanding of the salvation story." Wow... Yes Lord. This was going to be a huge day! God was preparing to do a mighty work today, and He has asked me to pray to prepare the way. How cool is that? Yes Lord... I will pray. I prayed for a while, until I felt, "It is done," In my spirit. I then grabbed my Bible and tip-toed back into my bedroom preparing to slip back into bed for a few more winks. About the time I laid my Bible back on the bedside table, I realized I was not going to get back into bed. That still small voice of the Holy Spirit said, "Get ready for work, you are going in to work early for Mr. Irwin."

By the time I had showered, dressed and was driving to the facility, the sun was just coming up. The sky was barely showing color when I left the house and after I had driven about 15 minutes the sky began to take on the blue color, showing it was going to be a beautiful day. As I drove, I continued to pray for God to lead me today for whatever His purpose would be. I was amazed that I felt so rested, since I was up hours earlier than my usual time of arising. In the midst of asking God what He wanted to say to Mr. Irwin when I arrived, that still small voice of the Holy Spirit said, "Tell him about the cross." OK, Lord, I can tell him about the cross. As I said this, my car had left the area of road which was covered by trees and I entered into a clearing at the top of a hill, which exposed the entire sky. The sudden transformation from leaving a darkened and shadowed area and driving into the light was awesome enough, yet in the sky, before my eyes, was a sight to be seen!

Before my eyes in the sky were three crosses. Three crosses! I immediately pulled my car to the edge of the road, unable to drive with my eyes full of tears. I was sobbing and sobbing with tears flowing as if the flood gates had opened. I kept wiping the tears away trying to see the crosses in the sky. The crosses were made from white vapors from airplanes. There were 3 parallel downward vapor lines and one vapor line crossing the entire three. The vapor lines did not extend much further than the crosses, nor were there any airplanes visible in the sky anywhere. Amazing! As I sat there looking at the crosses in the sky, that still small voice of the Holy Spirit said, "Tell him about the cross. Tell him about all three crosses." Yes, Lord, I will tell him about all three crosses. As I sat there looking at this amazing picture in the sky, I remembered that I had a camera in the car. I recently had the camera with me and I had left it in the car. I know it was not by chance that I had left the camera in the car. I retrieved the camera and took a picture of the three crosses in the sky. Thank you God for leaving the camera in the car so I could take this picture! You are so faithful. You knew that I would want this picture. OK, Lord, We need to go now... I have work to do. I can't wait to see Your plans for the day. Use me Lord!

I arrived at the facility about 5 AM that morning. I took my personal items into my office and then headed directly to Mr. Irwin's room. When I entered the room, Mr. Irwin turned his head and looked directly at me. "Well, Lord," I said out loud, "I see that you have already answered that prayer from earlier." As I walked toward the bed I smiled at Mr. Irwin and although he was unable to make his face muscles smile in return, he made a slight nod of his head. I knew that he had understanding and that God was healing his mind. I knew that God was healing his mind for the events that were going to happen today. I knew that I was going to tell Mr. Irwin about the crosses, and then I couldn't wait to see what God had planned for the rest of the day. "Use me Lord... tell me what to say," I thought as I approached the bed.

As I reached the bed, I gently ran my hand down the side of Mr. Irwin's face. "Good Morning champ," I said, "You've been a busy guy since I saw you yesterday. God's been healing your mind." Again, I got the same small nod. "God woke me up at 3 o'clock this morning just for you. Did you know that?" I asked. Again, there was a small nod of his head. About this time I was thinking, OK he's given 3 small nods with his head, do I even know that he's responding yes, or is he just moving his head slightly? I would need to ask a question that he may answer "No" with an alternate turning of his head. Let's try that, I thought. I need to know that his responses are appropriate. Next I asked, "Would you like me to leave now?" To this question, he slightly shook his head from side to side, indicating that he did not want me to leave. OK, Lord, now I know that he's responding properly.

I told Mr. Irwin that God had awakened me at 3 o'clock that morning to come and talk to him about the crosses. I asked him if he had ever heard the story about how Jesus died on the Cross for his sins. To this question, he nodded his head 'yes' and the nods were larger. He was able to move his neck a greater distance. Cool, I thought, God is doing something really awesome here. As I looked at Mr. Irwin, I couldn't help but see his pitiful condition. He had a tracheotomy in his neck through which he was breathing and the massive stroke had left him unable to move. I thought he must feel totally helpless. As I looked into his eyes, I could feel how much Jesus loves him and doesn't want him to die alone. I bent down closer and put my face very close to his while I looked into Mr. Irwin's eyes and said in a near whisper, "Do you know how much Jesus loves you? Do you know that He died on the cross for your sins? Do you know that He wants you to live in eternity with him?" I paused to see his reaction as his eyes filled up with tears. I got a tissue and wiped his tears, knowing that he was unable to wipe his own tears. He was nodding his head 'yes' now. Nodding his head repeatedly and not stopping. The nods were big. They were no longer slight nods. He was extending his neck as far as it would go, up and down. He was responding to the questions I had just asked him. He did know that Jesus loves him. He did know that Jesus died on the cross for his sins. He did know that Jesus wants him to be with him in eternity. That realization was a great first step.

As I stood there next to the bed amazed at his reaction and his physical improvement this morning, I was expecting someone else to enter the room. I stood there holding his hand, thinking that God would bring in a pastor to finish the job. I was thinking, OK God, this would be a good time now. He's ready. Then that still small voice of the Holy Spirit said, "Lead him in the sinner's prayer." ME, LORD? You want me to do that? Lord, I do not feel qualified to lead him. Then that some voice of the Holy Spirit said, "You are qualified. You know Me and I know you." I asked Mr. Irwin if he had ever heard about the sinner's prayer, and he nodded his head 'yes.' I asked him if he would like to say the sinner's prayer and he gently raised his hand off the bed and pointed his finger at me. He picked up his hand. He moved his hand! Now, that was pretty amazing! I looked at Mr. Irwin and said, "Now that was pretty amazing! I would call that a miracle! Yet, Salvation is the greatest miracle of all." I told Mr. Irwin that saying the sinner's prayer was not something I could do 'for' him. I told him, the words needed to come from his own mouth. I told him that I would say the words and that he could repeat them after me. I told him that since he couldn't speak or move his mouth, that he could just think the words after I said them and nod when he was finished, and I would continue. He nodded his head 'yes', that he would do that.

As I started the sinner's prayer, I said, "Dear Heavenly Father." He moved his lips and formed the words, "Dear Heavenly Father." There were no words coming out, but he was moving his lips. He was repeating the words. Just moments earlier that had not been possible. God had allowed his mouth to move to meet this need. Had Mr. Irwin only 'thought' the words, like I thought was going to happen, there would be no verification that the event had truly occurred. I would have had no way of knowing if he was thinking the words and repeating them in his mind after me, or merely just continuing to look at me. The prayer that was said earlier about his wife knowing and having assurance immediately came to my remembrance. How faithful is God to answer our prayers when we ask! I continued saying the sinner's prayer while Mr. Irwin moved his lips to each word. At the end, when we said Amen, he showed a small smile. There was a glow in his eyes and I knew that he was ready for what ever his maker had prepared for him. He had received Jesus as his personal savior. I said to him, "Where is Jesus?" and he raised his hand to his chest and patted his chest. Praise God! Mr. Irwin received Jesus as his personal savior on March 1, 2002.

It was my joy to tell Mrs. Irwin when she arrived at the nursing home that morning about God awakening me early, instructing me to pray, coming to work early, and seeing the three crosses in the sky. Mrs. Irwin danced in her husband's room that morning praising her Lord, when I told her that her husband had accepted Jesus as his personal savior that morning. When she looked at her husband and asked him what had happened that morning, he mouthed the word, 'Jesus' and patted his chest. It had been the diligence of a praying wife for her husband's soul that had made all the difference. She had prayed for many years for her husband and God had been faithful to honor your prayers.

God is faithful to answer our prayers for our loved ones who need salvation. I am so thankful that God used me that day. He could have easily allowed someone else who was more qualified to assist, yet I needed to have my faith built that day. It does not take a pastor to lead someone to Christ, only a willing vessel.

John 3:16

For God so loved the world that He gave His one and only Son, that whoever believes in Him shall not perish but have eternal life.

Chapter 19

The Clock stood still

✝

For a three year period, I worked for an Assisted Living Company. This was a refreshing break from the Nursing Home Industry, as the residents were at a higher level of physical functioning and the facilities were much nicer. Assisted Living facilities have nice carpet, decorations, chandeliers, and overall just a more elegant environment. My position as regional support also meant that in the event of a management position vacancy, I would assume that role until a replacement could be found. Occasionally, it is necessary to terminate someone's employment due to poor performance, and if that position was a high level management position, I would just step in and complete the job duties until I could hire a replacement for that particular position. While filling one such position in an Assisted Living facility, I was not within a reasonable driving distance from my home, so I was actually staying in a hotel for several weeks while assuming the job duties of that management position in the facility. I had interviewed several candidates and had not yet found the candidate whom I felt would be the perfect fit for that facility. Although I wanted to be relieved of the position duties myself, I wanted to be sure that the person I placed into this facility management position would be successful, so I was not going to hire just anyone.

I was encouraged to review a resume from a candidate who seemed to be a perfect fit for the position. I had completed an initial telephone interview and determined that a face-to-face interview needed to be conducted immediately. She sounded perfect and I didn't want to lose the opportunity to 'grab-her up' before anyone else. The healthcare industry is running short on healthcare professionals, so anyone with experience and a good track-record needs to be captured immediately. I set up an interview for the following day and prayed that this candidate would be the perfect fit for which I had been praying. During the initial telephone interview, the candidate had mentioned that she has a 'problem' with inconsiderate people and had in the past left a facility while waiting for an interview, since she had been made to wait an extended period of time. I understood her frustration and assured her that her interview would be conducted in a timely matter.

The interview was scheduled for 11:00 AM. I had already advised the receptionist to hold all my calls and to take messages, so I could return calls later, upon completion of the interview. I had completed my facility rounds and was back in my office by 10:50 AM awaiting the arrival of my candidate. I was so excited and couldn't wait for her arrival, since I felt in my spirit she would be the one I hired. At 10: 58 AM an elderly male resident rolled his wheelchair up to the entrance of my office door, and asked if he could come in and speak with me. At the same moment, the receptionist was standing behind him, motioning to me that my candidate was in the front lobby waiting for her interview. I was about to tell the resident that I had an interview and would speak with him after that was completed. Yet, his next words, stopped me in my tracks, and changed my plans. This elderly male resident, whom was about 80 years old, said, "I want to talk with you about Jesus. You said there was a way that I could receive him as my personal savior." Yes indeed, I had spoken with this resident about Jesus. It was common for me to make rounds and talk to the residents about Jesus. From working there for several weeks, I knew who was saved and who was not saved. I was praying for several to receive Jesus as their personal savior.

There he sat in front of me, in his wheelchair, asking permission to come into my office. This could not have been at a worse time for me, as I had a candidate sitting in the lobby waiting to be interviewed. She had a previous experience of having to wait for an extended period of time and had walked out of that facility, having felt like she was not respected. As this thought was flashing through my mind, I knew the only decision I could make. Jesus had to come first over all other things. Bringing one soul into the kingdom of heaven was more valuable than hiring any candidate. This was his time and how could I know that he would be provided another opportunity. Life is uncertain and he may have passed away before I had completed that interview. Although these thoughts were racing through my mind, there was never a hesitation, as I motioned to the receptionist that there would be a delay in the interview. I told the male resident that I was surely never too busy to talk about Jesus, as I pushed his wheelchair into my office and closed the door. As I was sliding a chair up beside him, so we cold talk, I said silently, "Lord You know my heart. Jesus comes first. You also know there is a candidate in the lobby that I don't want to leave. Please make this time be 'God-speed' timing. Let this event happen quickly so the other duties which I have to perform today will not be impaired."

As the male resident started to speak I glanced up at the clock. It was exactly 11:00 AM. Like most elderly people, who start their story from the beginning, he started talking about going to church as a child. I remember thinking, 'this is going to take a long time.' He spoke about his parents being Christians, about his brothers and sisters, and about going to Sunday school as a child. He spoke about his Father being an elder of the church and one brother that went on to be a preacher. He talked about getting married in the church and how his wife, who loved Jesus, had passed away several years ago. He talked on and on, and although I never looked back at that clock which was positioned over the door, I knew at least 30 minutes had passed. He said that when I had spoken with him about accepting Jesus as his personal

Savior and when I had commanded the enemy to "take off any blinders which had prevented him from seeing the truth," he had realized that he never said anything for himself to make that decision. We talked about the cross and God's plans for our lives. By this time, I had relaxed and was enjoying the conversation, since I was sure my candidate was long gone.

As I lead this sweet man to the Lord, I said the sinner's prayer and he repeated each word with reverence and complete faith. He was so excited and he said that he had finally "seen the light." It was glorious to see his sweet man praising God for allowing him to live long enough to make the decision. He glanced at his watch and said, "Oh dear, I have kept you an hour. I am sorry. I know that you must have lots off stuff to do." I assured him, that nothing was more important that adding someone to the Lord's service. As he turned his wheelchair to leave the room, I glanced at the clock for the first time since I had started our conversation. The hands on the clock sat at exactly 11:00AM. I thought the batteries have died exactly at 11:00AM. What is the chance that the batteries would die at exactly at 11:00AM? How odd! As he exited the room, I also left the office. My plans were to speak with the receptionist to find out what the candidate had said when she left the facility. I had hopes that she would have understood that I was in my office with a resident and that the resident's needs must always come first.

As I entered the lobby a well dressed female arose from her chair and approached me as she introduced herself. She was the candidate. She was still here. She had not left the facility. 'Amazing,' I thought. As I shook her hand, I thanked her for waiting and apologized for being late to our appointment. She smiled and said, "Late? You are right on time. It's exactly eleven o'clock." I glanced at the clock above the receptionist's desk and saw that the clock hands were precisely set on eleven o'clock. We chatted as we walked back to my office, which was the first door past the lobby. As I walked into the office, I gestured toward the chair for her to sit as I closed the door behind us. I glanced up at the clock hanging over the door and noted that the hands were now sitting at 11:01 AM. The hands were moving now. Had the time actually stood still the entire time I was with the resident? Had that request for God to use 'God-speed' time actually been the cause for time to stand still? I was really amazed that I had just experienced talking to someone for an hour, yet time had stood still. I thanked the candidate for coming and asked her how long she had waited to see me after she had arrived. As she said, "I had barely sat down when you came out," I could feel the anointing all over me and every hair on my body felt electrified. I had just experienced the supernatural act of God making time stand still. The Bible says that his time is not our time and now I realize that is true. I still may not totally understand it, but I know God's time is very different from ours. I know that if we say "yes" to God, He can make it all fit in our time constraints. All we need to do is ask for his help. I know that had I not asked for 'God-speed' timing, it would have been an hour long process.

I did hire the candidate I interviewed that day. Not only was she the perfect fit for the facility based on her experience, but she shared with me that she was a Christian and that God had directed her to apply at that facility. Isn't it just like God to show up and show off?

Praise God! To God be all the Glory! Praise God!

Proverbs 16:9

In his heart a man plans his course, but the Lord determines his steps.

Chapter 20

You want me to call her at midnight?

✝

I was a nurse consultant for a long term care company and had an assignment working in a specific facility in another state for several months. While working in that facility I worked long hours and since the distance was beyond an easy commute from my home, I stayed in a hotel during the week and only returned home on weekends. It was a 'clean up' job for a nursing home facility they had recently purchased. The company had realized after the purchase that the facility was indeed in really bad shape. They needed someone with extensive clinical experience to go in and turn the facility around. I said 'yes' to the challenge knowing that the task would require extensive commitment and long hours.

Most nights I would return to my hotel from the facility around eleven o'clock and fall into bed, exhausted from the long day's work. This practice had gone on for several weeks and it was beginning to take its toll on me physically when I cried out to the Lord one night to 'refresh me.' Not only had the long hours affected me physically by making me exhausted, it had also prevented my normal routine to spend time in God's word. I was praying daily and asking for his intervention with each project, yet I was not taking the time to read the word. Sleep had become my greatest commodity and to be perfectly honest, I hadn't given the Bible much thought during those weeks. No sooner had I cried out to God to 'refresh me,' that night as I returned to the hotel room at eleven o'clock, He said back to me, "You haven't listened for My voice or read My word in weeks. You have asked for My intervention constantly and I have never let you down."

Oh, the terrible feeling of being reprimanded by your loving and faithful Heavenly Father! I had been so busy that I had become a whining spoiled rotten brat! All I had been doing was asking for him to intervene and to help me with all my tasks, yet I had not done anything for him. Weeks had gone by and I had not even picked up his word nor had I asked him to 'use me.' As I sat on the hotel bed weeping I asked God to forgive me. I asked God to 'Use me' and I would do 'whatever' He asked. I remember saying out loud, "Use me Lord! Use me Lord! Use me Lord!" I really don't know why I said that three times, I just felt that I had neglected Him so, that I really needed to mean it. I picked up my Bible from my suitcase and opened it blindly to a chapter and started reading. There were no bells and whistles coming from the topic I was reading. I remember that I was reading from the New Testament, yet didn't write in my journal what chapter I was reading that night.

I had read the Bible for a short time that night when I heard that still small voice of the Holy Spirit say, "Call Stacy." I pondered that request for a few seconds, and then asked, "Lord, do you really want me to call Stacy now? It's midnight. Can I call her first thing in the morning? She has children who will wake up if I call the house at this hour." I waited for his response... quiet... quiet... quiet... no response. I looked at the clock again. Yes, it was midnight. Yes the children would be all asleep by now. It was a school night and she had four sleeping boys. I waited no longer, since God was not responding, it was apparent that He did want me to call her at this time. Stacy is a friend from the church with whom I had become close friends. As I dialed the phone to call Stacy I hoped that the phone ringing would not wake her children or her husband. As I was dialing the phone, God said, "Tell her ... to tell her husband ... get in the bath tub... as hot as he can stand it." As these words were coming from the Holy Spirit... I could hear 'pop rocks.' For those of you who are older, you will remember the small candy pieces called 'Pop-Rocks' which when put into your mouth would pop and snap. The candy had some kind of gas that was released when wet, to make the candy snap and pop in your mouth. That's the sound that I was hearing in my ear. Was it phone static? No... it was a sound God was allowing me to hear. But, why?

Stacy picked the phone up on the second ring and I was sure she would be upset with this late night phone call. She said, "Hello." My mind raced as she spoke into the phone. She's going to think I am crazy! Calling someone at midnight is beyond crazy, I thought.

"Stacy, I am so sorry to be calling you so late," I said apologetically, "I hope I didn't wake anyone else up. I know that it's midnight. I'm sorry to wake you at this hour."

"Oh, no," Stacy said, "You didn't wake me up. I was awake with my husband. It's OK."

"Well," I started, "God wanted me to call you. He wants me to tell you something. Tell your husband to get in the bath tub just as hot as he can stand it." "And Stacy," I added, "I'm hearing pop rocks snap and crackle. I'm not sure what that has to do with it. I feel like I'm supposed to tell you that too."

"Thank you Helena," she said, "Wait a minute." In the back ground I could hear her telling her husband to run the bath tub just as hot as he could stand it. When she came back to the phone, she told me that she had been up with her husband at that hour, because he was feeling so sick. Stacy said that he had never felt so sick and that his stomach was bloated so large that he looked like he was nine-months pregnant. "Thank you so much for calling and giving God's word," she said, "We really needed that. We were just thinking that he would need to go to the hospital tonight and we really cannot afford that. Just moments before you called, we were crying out for God to intervene." She excused herself and said that she needed to go, so she could help her husband get into the bath tub.

As I hung up the phone I thanked God for using me to help Stacy's husband tonight. They were calling out to God and God used me. God could have easily told them what to do, but He used me... to bless me! I laid my head on the pillow and drifted off to sleep, thanking God for the Blessing. I had been totally wrapped up in the worldly needs, yet when I asked God to 'Use me' it was like I had never drifted away. He never moved... I was the one who had moved. He had remained right there waiting on me to return. I fell asleep telling Jesus how much I love him.

I awoke suddenly... what was that? Something was ringing. As I came to my senses, I realized that it was my cell phone ringing. As I grabbed for my cell phone on the bed-side table, I was facing the alarm clock and could see the time was 1:30 AM. I remember thinking there must be something wrong at the nursing home and I would have to go back there at this hour. "Hello, this is Helena, How may I help you," I said. "This is Stacy. I am so sorry to call you at this hour," she said, "I know that you must have been asleep." I admitted that I had been asleep, yet was grateful that it was not the nursing home. We both laughed that I had thought it was the nursing home calling and I told her that I had called her at midnight, so this was only fair to get a call back. Stacy was so excited that she just had to call me and she knew that I would want to know how her husband was feeling. "Yes," I said, "I do want to know. Tell me what happened." Stacy told me that she had helped her husband into the very hot bath tub and he had sat there for several minutes. She said that the very hot bath tub was exactly what he needed. After several minutes, he started passing gas. Stacy laughed. She said, "He was passing lots of tiny bubbles and the entire tub was full of popping and snapping bubbles. It sounded like those

'Pop-Rocks' you heard. He did this for a long time and his stomach flattened right down. His bloated stomach had been full of gas and now it's all gone. All the bloating and pain is gone." We said a few "Praise God" then hung up the phones to get some sleep.

God is so faithful to 'use us' when we ask. God will wait patiently when we are busy and during times when we live our life without him. God will resume his intimate relationship with you, when you realize your mistake and ask forgiveness. God will never 'make' you do something. As His children; He is patient and waits for our obedience. God loves us too much to cast us aside. He is patient with his children.

Praise God! To God be all the Glory!

John 14:12-14

"I tell you the truth; any one who has faith in me will do what I am doing. He will do even greater things than these, because I am going to the father. And I will do whatever you ask in my name, so that the Son may bring glory to the Father. You may ask me for anything in my name, and I will do it."

Chapter 21

She had rheumatoid arthritis for years

†

Since attending our latest non-denomina-tional church for the past two years we had sat in relatively the same area. My husband and I had always been attracted and drawn to sit in the front left side of every church we have attended, in the second row from the front. I am not sure why this area had always attracted us, yet never-the-less, there we sit, and stand, and praise. In this particular church we again sit in the second row, although when someone else is sitting there upon our arrival, we sit elsewhere without saying a word. I'm sure you have been to churches, where those seats are claimed by other people and you were informed that you were in someone else's seat. I had been to some places like that. My husband and I are not like that. We will sit anywhere without making a fuss. This new church we had attended for the past two years is only starting to grow in the gifts of the spirit and we know that God had placed us there for the growth which is yet to come. The preaching is great and the worship is out-of this world. We must be willing vessels to be used by God wherever He wants to use us, even if that means changing churches to be 'used' elsewhere.

When Fred and I are planning our vacations, we always ask God where he would have us to go. We have found over the years, that by asking God, He will 'use' us even on vacation. One year when we were praying where we were to take our vacation we both clearly heard God directing us to Montana. That year we had planned a vacation for October and I was concerned that it would be really cold in Montana in October. We were scheduling a vacation for the last week in October, when God said "Montana" we joked about God allowing us to leave New Jersey for warmer weather, yet now takes us to Montana on vacation. We booked the condo and air arrangements for an area in western Montana with no clear direction as to what God had up his sleeve for this vacation. For several weeks prior to our vacation I had been searching the internet for churches in the area which we could attend. We always enjoyed attending other churches on vacation and I liked doing the research prior to arrival in the area, so we always knew where we would be going to church while on vacation. I have often heard other Christians say that they don't attend church on vacation, since they are on vacation; they feel they are also on vacation from church. Fred and I have always enjoyed attending church on vacation. Our children were raised with the excitement of various churches as being part of the vacation adventure. As I researched the churches in the area of Montana where we would be on vacation, there were several non-denominational churches, yet none jumped out at me as being 'the one.' A few days before we were leaving, I went on the internet again and repeated the search for a church in the area. I felt that God was directing me to search again. I felt like the fisherman in the Bible who had fished all night without caching any fish and Jesus told him to cast his net again. I remember saying to God, "Yes, Lord, I'll do this again." WOW. There it was. This time the search showed another non-denominational church that had not previously been listed. It was a newly developed church web site for a church which was relatively new. As soon as I saw the name of the church, I knew that was it. That was the church we were supposed to attend and also our 'reason' for vacationing in Montana. We flew into Montana on Saturday afternoon and we checked out the location of the church first thing, so we knew where we would be going in the morning. When I woke up on Sunday morning God told me that a baby needed to be healed in that church and another "Mother" had a great burden. Moments later when Fred woke up, I asked him if he had received any word from God about any needs for the church and to my amazement, he reported there was a baby in the church that needed healing. Yes, indeed, we were vacationing in Montana for this baby's healing. Praise God. I was not given any other informa- tion about the "Mother" with a great burden, yet knew that God would reveal that when the time was right. As we drove into the church parking lot we were very excited to see what God was going to do. Before getting out of the car, Fred and I prayed for God's direction, the assurance of when to speak and for the Pastor to recognize why we were there. The church was very welcoming and the praise music was good. It was apparent that the church was very new and still stepping into authority and delegation of duties. As the praise was concluding, the pastor stood and announced there was "healing in the house" and those in need of healing or anyone with a word for healing was to come forward. The people looked around strangely, as if this had never occurred, and we knew that the pastor had heard from God. Fred and I walked down the side wall to the front and the pastor motioned for us to walk to the center. As I was about to give my word for healing a baby girl to the pastor, allowing him all authority, he handed me the microphone. I remember thinking, "he doesn't even know me or what I might want to say." Yet, he had obviously heard from God and had trust in what I would say. I called forth the baby that needed healing, and a father came forward with a small girl of no more than two years old. The father said that she had been sick since birth and they had cried out to God for her healing repeatedly. The frail little girl had apparent respiratory problems as her breathing was very loud and she was very pale. I asked the father if I could lay my hands on the child and got his permission before praying for her healing. My hands were so hot when I touched the child, I remember thinking it was going to burn the child. As the father turned to walk back to his seat with his child, the breathing was quiet and I knew she was fine. Next, I called forth the "Mother with a great burden." As a woman walked down the center aisle of the church from the back of the church toward me, God allowed me to see her burden. I remember thinking, "Oh my God. How can she handle that?" How could a Mother live with knowing that her husband had raped his own child and she was too ashamed to tell anyone about it? As she got closer, God allowed me to feel the burden she was feeling and as she got closer I stepped forward to meet her and I wrapped my arms around her and I cried with her. After she was able to speak, she said she couldn't speak out what her burden was because it was so horrible. I assured her that God had already told me and I gently whispered into her ear what God had told me and that He had allowed me to feel her burden and shame. She was in shock! God had told me? She said that it was so comforting to know that God loved her enough to help her through this terrible event. As I held her in my arms, I reminded her how much God loved her and that what had happened was not her fault. I was telling her what God was telling me. Although the event had happened years ago and the husband was no longer in the picture or any threat, her child would be fine and they both needed counseling. Her first step would be to talk to her pastor. She agreed and I walked her to her pastor. God's intervention that day was amazing. Allowing God to plan our vacations and 'use me' never gets old!

The gift of healing that God has placed upon me for his glory is only used when God directs. Healing is not a gift that I run around touching people by my own decision and in my own strength. The gift of healing is God's gift and therefore used at his direction and to his glory. It is not uncommon for people who know of the healing gift to call me and ask me to pray for them, knowing that I will ask God if He wants them to be healed through me. There have been times that God has advised me a particular illness is 'unto death,' and I know there should be no prayer for healing, but for comfort and peace. I would never tell someone that there illness is 'unto death' since we are to be an encouragement. When ever the Lord shows me that an illness is unto death, my focus turns to their salvation and assuring that they are ready for when that time comes to pass.

One Sunday, while in church, during singing praise, I felt the Holy Spirit telling me that I was supposed to 'touch the back' of the lady standing in front of me. I had spoken to this sweet lady on several occasions, yet I wasn't sure how she felt about a healing touch. I knew that I couldn't just touch her without asking first, and she was standing too far forward to speak with her without walking around in front of her, which would place me in front of her in the first row. "God, what do you want me to do? Can I do this immediately after church," I thought, "this would be very disruptive." I felt a gentle "yes," that God would allow it later. As the service finished, I walked around in front of the first row and touched her elbow to get her attention. She smiled as she turned around, and I told her that I felt like I was supposed to touch the center of her back, behind her heart and pray for her healing. I told her that I was not sure how she felt about healing or being touched. She said, "That would be great. You could have just done it." I placed my hand in the center of her back and prayed as God directed me for her healing. God told me to specifically say the "Heart." When I had finished praying, she said that her 'heart' had been giving her a lot of pain for several months and she was scheduled to have tests done the next day. She said the pain was totally gone now. Praise God. The next Sunday, she slid into her seat and announced that her heart was healed and she had no more pain after God had healed her. The music started and we were not able to talk any more. During the praise, God told me to pray for her again. I leaned forward and touched the middle of her back and felt that I was to pray for her "arthritis" to be healed. As I prayed, I was also told by the Holy Spirit to touch her upper, middle and lower back, hips and neck with my fingers reaching around to the front of her neck. The power surging through my hands was so strong; I could feel my entire body trembling. I knew that God was doing a mighty work. The following Sunday when she came into the church, she told me that she had arthritis really bad for years and she was not able to do many things. Yet, this past week, she had no pain and had been more flexible then she had been in many years. She knew that God had touched and healed her body. She said that she also knew that God had directed me to touch the front of her neck, to heal her "thyroid." She was proclaiming her total healing and had told all her friends in church about God's mighty work in her life. This happened in the new church we had been attending for two years and God was going to use her 'healing' to start the flow of miracles in the church.

Praise God! To God be all the Glory.

Luke 13: 10-13

On a Sabbath Jesus was teaching in one of the synagogues, and a woman was there who had been crippled by a spirit for eighteen years. She was bent over and could not straighten up at all. When Jesus saw her, He called her forward and said to her, "Woman you are set free from your infirmity." Then He put his hands on her, and immediately she straightened up and praised God.

Chapter 22

Leading other's to Christ

✝

God opened my heart to lead others to Christ on July 20, 1998 when my Grandfather accepted Jesus as his personal savior. That was such a glorious day for me that I felt like I could fly! Having the privilege of leading my Grandfather in saying the sinner's prayer was the highlight of my life. When people are asked about the best thing that ever happened in their lives they often recall their wedding day or the birth of their children as having been their best day. Prior to July 20,

1998 I had said the best day of my life had been my marriage to Fred in 1979 and the birth of my children in 1982 and 1984 and my receiving Jesus as my personal savior on October 24, 1984. Those were all glorious memories, yet they fade in comparison to the glory of leading someone to Jesus Christ. Until you have experienced the privilege of leading another person to receiving Jesus as their personal savior, you have not fulfilled your spiritual destiny. God has only allowed me the privilege because I asked him for that privilege. Do you think that statement sounds a bit crazy? People plant seeds all the time. The normal Christian will talk to their family and friends about Jesus and how He will change their lives and the promise of eternity in Heaven. I had done that for years and years myself. I was 'witnessing' to people who needed Jesus Christ and I was 'planting the seeds,' yet I had never taken the next step to actually tell them how they could do it or to help them to do it. Thinking back now, that seems a bit strange, that I never took the next step to helping them come to the Lord. I realize that I had been cautious all those years because I was insecure with my ability, since I did not know the Bible inside and out. There was a fear that they may ask something that I did not have the answer to. My prayer would always be, "Lord, send someone." I was praying that God would send someone to lead them to the Lord. How crazy was that? I was there and obviously had some type of relationship with the person, to even be talking about Jesus in the first place and I was praying for God to send someone else! Yet, on July 20, 1998 I realized that if I wanted my Grandfather to spend eternity with me in Heaven, I would have to be the one to help him. I had planted seeds into his life for years and now he was actually asking ME to help him do it. I had planned to 'talk about Jesus' again that day, yet he was ready. The Holy Spirit had prepared the way and he was ready that day to receive Jesus Christ as his personal savior. I thank God for that day as not only did He usher my Grandfather into his presence, yet He also opened my heart to leading others to Christ.

In the next few years that followed, God allowed me the privilege of leading twenty-two people to receive Jesus as their personal savior. That number may not seem like a great number, yet you must realize those 22 people were people I had contact with on a daily basis. The people that God allowed me the privilege to lead to the Lord were people that had been in church all their lives, for the most part. They were people who had prolonged making that decision and some who didn't realize there was a decision to be made at all. I had come to realize that there were many people, who although they were in church every Sunday, had never said the words themselves, to ask Jesus into their heart. Someone had prayed over them or they may have been 'dedicated' as a child to the church, and they thought they were ready. Isn't it just like the enemy to lie? The enemy will sit right next to you in a church pew and whisper in your ear that your soul is already going to Heaven and you don't need to do anything more about it. The enemy is here to lie, kill and destroy.

It was not an immediate conversion for me to lead others to Christ after my Grandfather's experience in July of 1998. The previous vision, I had only three months before in March of 1998, where people were being pushed over the edge of the Cliff into the fires of hell was still fresh in my memory. The vision was haunting and I could hear the screams of the people falling into the fires on hell. God would frequently replay the vision and I would hear over and over in my spirit, "Tell my people. Feed my sheep." One night, as I was going to bed, the vision flashed before my eyes again, and I begged God to show me a sweeter vision. The fires of hell were frightening and my heart was racing so, I couldn't handle it a moment longer. I told God, that He knew my heart and knew I wanted to please him. I asked God to show me 'who' needed to receive Jesus as their personal savior and I would do whatever He showed me. I asked for discernment to know and I asked for his words to lead them to Jesus Christ. That night I instantly saw a glorious vision. I was a huge field with white flowers. The field was as wide and long as my eyes could see and on the top of each plant the white flowers indicated the harvest was ready. Each plant represented a person who was ready to receive Jesus as their personal savior. God told my spirit, that others have planted the seeds into their lives and that they were ready. Others were praying to 'send someone' to finish the job. I smiled as I thought about how many times I had prayed that prayer myself, to 'send someone' to lead someone to Jesus. "Yes God," I prayed, "Use me."

In February of 1999 when I went to work that day in the nursing home, God opened my eyes to seeing who had already received Jesus as their personal savior and who was ready to receive Jesus as their personal savior. I was amazed that the discernment that I had asked to receive allowed me to see God's truth when I looked into their eyes. I had always known that the eyes are the window to the soul, yet now I was actually seeing into the condition of their souls. On the morning of February 5, 1999 while making my initial morning rounds I had the privilege of leading two precious people to receive Jesus as their personal savior. There was one man and one woman who received Jesus Christ as their personal savior that day and both were both over 80 years old. They were both regular church attendees and both had been children of pastors. Both had felt their salvation had been 'taken care of' by their earthly father. Both were cognitively intact and had full memory of their past and they both knew without a shadow of a doubt, they had never said the sinner's prayer or asked Jesus into their heart. Since they had both attended church, they already knew the Bible stories. They knew that Jesus had died on the cross for their sins and they knew the Bible pretty well. Their knowledge of the scriptures was actually much better then mine. They both had come dangerously close to not spending their eternity in Heaven. This day really opened my eyes to the need of the elderly. They were sweet and loving people who were living out their last days without Jesus Christ. I knew that the vision God had shown me of the harvest field full of white flowers ready for harvest was the elderly ready to receive Jesus as their personal savior. There was not much time. I knew their days were numbered and that I had much work to do.

I asked God, that these precious elderly people in my care, would not breath their last breathe until they had received Jesus Christ as their personal Savior. I prayed that prayer knowing that God would grant that prayer, since He had granted that prayer twice before. Over the months that followed the harvest was easy. Talking about Jesus had become easy and the elderly were always more then glad to talk with me about Jesus. On some days, God would allow me the privilege of leading two of my elderly residents to receive Jesus as their personal savior. It was amazing to see God's hand at work, as He would guide me to the people who were ready and who were prepared by the Holy Spirit to receive Jesus. It was the Holy Spirit's job to draw them. I had the easy part, since the Holy Spirit had already prepared their hearts.

"Tell me about the day you received Jesus as your personal savior?" That question would always open the door to their self realization. If they made a general comment about 'always' believing, I would ask them for the date they made their own decision and asked Jesus into their heart with their own mouth. I would then tell them my Salvation date, October 24, 1984, and let them know that date was the most important date in my life, since it assured my name was written in the 'Book of Life' and assured my place in Heaven. Then I would say, "If you can't recall a date, it didn't happen. The enemy is a liar and the great deceiver. He wants you to think you're 'already' on your way to heaven, so you don't actually make the decision." On a more personal note, I would tell them, "I want you to be in heaven with me, since I love you so much." You really can't get much more personal then that, and I truly did love them. When God opened my eyes by giving me discernment He also opened my heart and filled it with the love that He had for the lost as well. I did want them to be in Heaven with me, the same as God wants them to be in Heaven with him.

In those early years, I would list the name of each person I had the privilege of leading to the Lord in the back of my Bible. There were multiple blank pages in the back of my Bible, and it just seemed like the perfect place to write down the names that 'I had the privilege to lead to the Lord.' I would pray for them and ask God to use them to reach their family. One day in August of the year 2000 as I was writing a name in the back pages of my Bible, as I had been doing for 3½ years, the Lord asked me why I was doing that. "Well, Lord," I explained, "I really don't know." 'Yes you do know,' the spirit said back to me. "Well, I suppose I am keeping a list," I replied as I started to weep, as I felt the Holy Spirit grieving. I was keeping a list, as if I had anything to do with it. God made it very clear that day, that He was already writing the names into the 'Book of Life' and I was to stop keeping my list. I stopped adding to the list that day, except for my family members that were added to the Kingdom. I had grieved the Holy Spirit and I never wanted to feel that again. It was a deep internal feeling of sorrow like I had never felt before. My work continued and intensified as I gave God all the Glory for drawing people to salvation.

Praise God! To God be all the glory forever and ever Amen!

John 4:38

"I sent you to reap what you have not worked for. Others have done the hard work, and you have reaped the benefits of their labor."

Chapter 23

Authority in Heaven

✝

I cannot stress enough, the importance of writing a personal spiritual journal. I had never been one to write a diary, and actually thought it was a 'silly' idea to write down your thoughts where someone could later read your most private and inner-most thoughts. In 1997 I heard a woman on Christian television talk about the importance of 'journaling' your spiritual walk, that you can re-read to remember words God has given you and see your spiritual growth over the years. This really clicked for me when she said that, and within the week, I had purchased my first journal. On June 7, 1997 I made my first entry into that journal and have been journaling since. I have gone through several journals since then and when I read back in those old journals, I am able to clearly see my spiritual growth and times that God has used me to His glory. I am not faithful to write in my journal daily, yet when I do write in my journal, God is always faithful to allow me to recall events that I should record. My journal entries include words God has given me through his scripture, words He has given to me through other people, and times that God has used me to encourage someone, witness about Jesus, or pray healing. After a recent move into our new home, I realized that I am missing one large journal covering the period from 2000 to 2004 and I am praying that God will allow me to locate that particular journal as it also contains the picture of the three crosses in the sky. My journals have become precious memories and I expect them to be joyous sentimental treasures for my children when I pass on to be with my Heavenly Father.

On Sunday May 15, 2005 I had an experience which changed my life forever and is included in my personal journal. The experience I am about to recall changed my view of what people do in Heaven and changed my view of where prayer is most effective. The event that I am about to share with you so changed my life that I was unable to speak about it for weeks. Each time that I tried to share the experience, I would become so overwhelmed with God's amazing love that I would just start crying uncontrollably and would be unable to speak. It would be weeks before I was able to share the experience with a sister in Christ, at which time the spirit of God fell and she also cried uncontrollably with me.

The morning of May 15, 2005 I awoke at 8:30 AM. I knew that I was not feeling well and could not put on finger on where I was not feeling well that morning. I felt sick, yet I pushed myself to get out of bed. It was Sunday and I loved going to church. God was mighty in my life and I loved to see what He had up his sleeve at church. There was always a word to give or encouragement needed, and I loved God to use me. Sundays in our home are always very special, since this is the one day of the week that my husband Fred rises early and makes breakfast for the family. He loves to make breakfast on Sunday mornings and he continues the practice to this day. On that particular morning Fred had made bacon and eggs, and although I don't remember that fact now, it was in my journal. While I was eating my breakfast I started getting a pain in my right side of my abdomen and as I continued to eat, the intensity of the pain got worse. By the time I had finished my breakfast the pain had become unbearable and I had started to sweat profusely. I left the breakfast table and immediately lay down on my bed, as the pain increased and I started to chill, knowing that I must also have a high temperature. The pain has become so intense that I was finding it very difficult to even move onto my side in the bed. I pushed myself up from the bed to go into the bathroom and check my temperature. It was 102 degrees. Returning to bed I wrapped up in my blanket and prayed for God to remove this pain. Being a nurse, I knew that pain in the right side of the abdomen could be appendicitis, and with the severe pain and high temperature I was sure that was the problem. As Fred came into the bedroom I told him that there was no way I could go to church and I told him about the extreme pain and my high temperature. I remember thinking that I felt too sick to sit up and go to the hospital. God would have to provide. Before long, Fred appeared from the bathroom completely dressed and ready to go to church. I was surprised that Fred was going to church without me, since I was so sick, yet there he was all dressed and ready to leave. I asked Fred to pray for me, and he said, "Will do," and left the bedroom. I lay in the bed crying after Fred left the house and I was asking God why Fred did not understand that I needed him to pray for me then. Why had Fred left me? I felt so abandoned and felt like he didn't care enough about me. He had just left me and went on to church. I remember feeling so sick and sore, crying, sweating… Next thing I remember was being in a 'dream-like' state. I was not awake and I was not sleeping either. I could feel no pain. I could feel no breathing.

I felt peaceful. I was not in my body. I was not sure where I was, but I knew that I was not in my bedroom. I was floating in an upright position and to my left I could see my father; Leon, my mother-in-law; Alma, and my father's brother; Myron. All I remember seeing is their faces and I couldn't see any background to know where I was. My Father and my mother-in-law had passed away just weeks of each other in 1999. My father had passed away on July 5, 1999 and my mother-in-law had passed away on March 21, 1999. My uncle had passed away on September 21, 1997. I was in the presence of people who had already passed away. All three were looking at me and not saying a word. Their faces were 'studying' me. They were serious and not smiling. I asked why they were not smiling. Although I did not see Jesus, I heard him say, "They accepted my gift of Salvation, but did nothing to bring any souls to my Kingdom. They have no voice and they have been given no authority." The voice had come from behind me and I knew that Jesus was standing directly behind me. I floated a short distance forward and came to more people on my left side. These next people were all smiling and all able to speak. The first face I saw on my left side was my Papa. Papa said, "Cookie, I have been given authority over Fred's anger." It was Papa's voice. Although Papa did not phys-ically touch me, I could feel his love envelop me. The next face on my left was Aunt Helen (Fred's cousin). Aunt Helen said, "Hi Sugar. I have been given authority over your marriage." Again, I felt the love wrapped around me. The next person on the left was Ray. Ray was an elderly man in our church whom had been a preacher. Ray said, "Hi dear. I was your son's spiritual father for a season on earth. I was given authority over your son's learning disability and his spouse." Again, love surrounded me. Next on my left side appeared Nelda. Nelda was an elderly woman from our church, who had been married to Ray. Nelda said, "I loved your daughter on earth and we watched wedding shows together. I have authority over her spouse." Next on my left side was my Grandmother (My father's Mother), Delci. She said, "Hi Honey. I have prayed my family into the Kingdom and you are the first to win souls. You have personally lead 46 people into the Kingdom and 148 others made the choice due to your example. I am so proud of you. I have authority over your health. The enemy has attacked frequently due to your fruit. You will be fine. Your time is not yet. You have much work to do." As I could feel her love all around me, I also became very aware that I was drifting back and away from her. I asked her, "Who has authority over my finances?" She was smiling at me, yet not saying anything in response to my question. Then I heard the voice of Jesus saying, "That authority has not yet been given." Suddenly I was back in my body and I could still hear my Grandmother's voice saying, "I am sending a faithful servant to pray healing. You will be fine now."

As I lay there back in my body, the pain was not as intense as it had been earlier although I knew that the temperature was still very high, as I was still very sweaty. It wasn't a moment later that my daughter Jessica came into my bedroom. "Mommy," she said, "Are you sick?" I looked up at her and knew that she was the 'faithful servant' that my grandmother had said would come to pray healing for me. "Yes," I said back to Jessica. "Can I pray for you?" she asked. "Yes," I said, as I placed her hand on the right side of my abdomen. As she prayed the pain disappeared completely. After she left the room, I got out of bed and check my temperature. My temperature was now 99 degrees. I rechecked my temperature a few minutes later, at which time my temperature was a normal 98.6 degrees. In my spirit I could hear the words, "Rest…Rest…Rest." I stayed in bed resting for the next 4 hours as I reflected on what had happened that morning. I knew that God had intervened on the enemy's plan to kill me that morning. Praise God for his intervention. All the events that I had experienced were reeling around in my mind. I now knew that when people go to Heaven, they get authority over areas, if they had added to the Kingdom when they were on earth. As I reflected on what I had just learned, it all made perfect sense. Papa had passed away 6 years earlier and Fred's mood had been amazingly transformed. He used to be easily angered, yet now he was more even-tempered. Our marriage was awesome in the past few years, since Aunt Helen had passed away. David's learning disability had suddenly disappeared after Ray's death. I knew that my health would be attacked, yet knew there was Heavenly authority assigned to my health. Over the next 2 weeks I rested in the words I had heard and the love I felt that morning. The love that had enveloped me was intense and I realized that the love I had felt had been transferred to my spirit. The feeling of spirit-to-spirit love was so much more intense than any physical touch. It had been so comforting to hear their voices. With refection of what they said, I also realized that I was addressed by the nick-name they had used on earth. I was never called by my given name, Helena, but I was called by the individual name they had used on earth. Nelda had just started talking without using any type of nick-name and I realized that was how she spoke to me when she was alive. She just started talking without using any type of name. Papa had called me 'Cookie,' which was the name he had called me since my childhood. No matter how many times I had protested as I got older, he continued to call me 'Cookie.' As I got older, I surrendered to his request and referred to my self as 'Cookie' when I called him on the phone, and I could hear him smile across the phone.

Days later, I asked my daughter about the days she sat with Nelda before her death. Her husband, Ray had passed away before Nelda, and not wanting her to be alone, my daughter had agreed to sit with Nelda during the day that summer, while her son was at work. Jessica reported that they just watched TV most of the time and that Nelda was a sweet good Christian woman. I asked Jessica what they watched on TV and she responded, "She loved to watch those wedding shows. We watched them everyday. She would talk about how God provides the perfect spouse if we wait on him to provide. She said that God has the perfect husband waiting for me." They watched wedding shows. Wow! Not that I doubted what Nelda said to me that Sunday morning, yet it's always wonderful to hear confirmation. I never knew that that Nelda and Jessica had watched wedding shows everyday nor did I know that Nelda had spoken with her about God having the perfect husband waiting for her. I was happy that Jessica had agreed to sit with Nelda that summer, yet I had never asked her what they watched on TV or what they had talked about for that matter.

A few days later, I asked my son David about his relationship with Ray. David would often visit Ray with another member of our church to help do things around the house that Ray was no longer able to do at his age. David said that

Ray was a wonderful man and that Ray would often give him "words of advice for living a good life." David said, "He was like a father to me." David went on to say, that Ray had become his "Spiritual Father." WOW! More confirmation.

I prayed and asked God to assign that Authority for my finances. Money was really tight during that time and I could not understand why the authority over my finances was not yet assigned. That was a huge need and I just could not figure out why there was not heavenly authority given for our finances. I prayed about the areas that had authority in Heaven and was determined that God would reveal an answer. I was like a spoiled rotten little brat repeatedly asking my Heavenly Father… "Show me… tell me… what do I need to do?" The answer suddenly dropped into my spirit after about two weeks of refection. I was amazed that the common denominator for all areas that had authority in Heaven was the church ALTAR! Could that be it? I had gone to the altar at church and prayed and gave those areas to God! I had gone forward to the church altar for Fred's anger, our marriage, David's learning disability, David's spouse selection, Jessica's spouse selection, and my health. The altar! That was it! The altar is where we present our sacrifice. It's where we lay it all down and give God all our stuff. Until we lay it down, He can not do anything for that area in our lives. He allows us to have our own will, and until we lay down each individual concern or need, it remains our problem. Wow! What a revelation! If people knew this, the church altars would be packed full every time the doors were open. As I was reflecting on this revelation, the spirit spoke, "feed my sheep." I responded, "Yes... Lord... I will tell them." The next Sunday I was in front of my church sharing my testimony and the altar was full. I was there too! That first Sunday after my revelation I was at the altar giving God my finance problems. I know that God has assigned Heavenly authority over my finances, because things have turned around. Not that there are never money concerns now, yet it no longer keeps me awake at night. God always provides and I know that our obedience through the hard times while continuing to tithe pleases God. I have wondered who has been assigned that authority. I smile when I think about the possibility of my Mother having authority over my finances. She passed away after I gave my finances to God at the church altar and she may have been assigned that authority.

I have often heard people say that it will be boring in Heaven with nothing to do but praise God. I now have a new outlook on what happens in Heaven. We will have assigned duties and responsibilities in Heaven. It will be a glorious time to gather with all of our friends and loved ones whom have gone home before us. I would love to see you there! I want to know that you will be with me in eternity! Have you made that decision to receive Jesus as your personal savior? Do you remember the date? Don't trust your eternity on anyone else… Speak the words for yourself. Ask Jesus into your heart. Then take all your problems to the altar and give them all to God. Let it all go and feel your freedom in Christ.

Praise God! To God be all the Glory forever and ever. Amen.

Mathew 28:18
"All Authority in Heaven and on earth has been given to me."

Mathew 16:19

"I will give you the keys of the Kingdom of heaven; whatever you bind on earth will be bound in Heaven, and whatever you loose on earth will be loosed in Heaven."

Chapter 24

New levels/ new spiritual warfare

Allowing God to 'Use' me has not come without trials and spiritual warfare. If you do not know what 'spiritual warfare' is, then you have never followed the teachings of Jesus Christ with all your heart, mind and soul. When the enemy knows that you love Jesus Christ and are working to bring people into his kingdom, he will try everything to stop you. The enemy is the great deceiver and he will use people to say lies about you and make people question your character. Over the years

I have had lies said against me both in my professional career and in my personal life. The enemy can take a simple comment and twist it into something that makes you look like a non-Christian. The enemy wants nothing more than to 'disqualify' your actions, so that people will not see you as a faith-living Christian. The more intense your commitment becomes to leading people to accept Jesus Christ as their personal savior, the more intense your spiritual warfare becomes. In times when I had slacked off, due to pure exhaustion from the spiritual warfare, everything settles down and life becomes smooth and easy without any stress or hardship. That is the enemy's plan... to stop you from working for the progression of the Kingdom. I have realized over the years, that during times of no concerns and trials, I am not fulfilling my duty as a Christian. If you are not on the enemy's radar you are not doing your job.

There will be spiritual warfare, so I have adjusted to knowing that fact. I have also adjusted my prayer life to cover and protect myself and my family from the attacks that will come. When the enemy is unable to 'get your attention,' he will try to attack your children. The enemy knows that your children are your heart, so he will try to discourage you from following Christ by allowing your children to be attacked. As a parent, it is natural to want your children to be safe, so he expects you will back down when he starts messing with them. My husband and I start each day praying for our family members individually. We pray protection over each one specifically. We ask God to place His protective angels around each one to keep them from harm. We pray that they will hear God's voice in all circumstances and will have a greater discernment for any evil which may come their way. God is faithful to answer prayers when they are said with faith in knowing His will for our lives.

Over my career I have lost three jobs through untrue statements being said about something I had said or done. Although the enemy used people to commit these acts, the Lord has always been faithful to uphold my values and character, and prevent me from seeking retaliation. It is human nature to want to make the truth know, yet in doing so, it often makes the victim appear guiltier. Nothing can be accomplished through whining and blaming others. What is done is done. It is what it is! I am always reminded of the meek and humble posture Jesus held when falsely accused. He had the ability to strike them down yet He knew there would be greater things to come by allowing the situation to continue to fulfillment. The Holy

Spirit has always comforted my soul in my times of these trials and the result has always been a greater promotion both in my profession, in my personal life and in the Kingdom. Although the job losses came totally unexpected and left me feeling devastated, God's plan was to remove me from those situations, which was later revealed. In all situations there was something un-Godly occurring in the organization in which God did not want me to be associated. What the enemy had planned for failure was used by God for promotion. Isn't it just like God to make lemonade from lemons? We must always trust that God has a greater plan for our lives and that God truly does know best!

Praying protection for ourselves, our family members and our homes allows God to provide the needed protection. When I look back over events in our family, it was the grace of God's protection that prevented tragic outcomes from occurring. In an earlier chapter I told of the tornado coming to our property line and making a 90 degree turn. That would not have occurred had it not been for our prayer over the property for protection and our giving that property to God. In another situation, my son was driving home from high school on a cold winter day. An ice storm on the previous day had left the roads icy and as he was traveling around a curve his Bronco left the road and crashed head-on into a tree. The enemy had plans to harm my son that day, yet with prayers of protection over my son, God's protection prevented my son from being harmed. Although he hit that tree hard enough to push the hood entirely up to the windshield, there was not a scratch on his body. My son David had his Bible on his back seat from having attended church days prior to the accident, and upon impact his Bible flew forward from the back seat and landed wide-open in front of him on the dash. Now, what is the chance that anything like that would happen? I would expect it would have hit the back of the front seat and landed on the floor. A Bible flying up over the seat and over David's head and land on the dash, that is God showing his presence! Don't you just love it when God shows up and shows off? When David told me of this amazing 'Bible flying' event, I asked him what chapter the Bible had opened to. He had no idea what book or chapter it had opened to, because he just grabbed that Bible up and thanked God for ... protection! He also tells of the "hand" that held his right shoulder back upon impact. His seat belt came across his left shoulder, yet he could feel a very definite "hand" on his right shoulder holding him tightly into his seat. I don't think that Bible came flying from the back seat at all that day! I believe it was picked up and placed on the dash by the person who was holding him tightly. I just love God! Don't you?

In another amazing event, my husband Fred was working in a tobacco field several years ago. We no longer grow and sell tobacco, yet back then it was a significant source of income for our family. During the growing process the plants develop a bunch of seed pods on the top which need to be cut off to allow the plant to fully develop and increase in weight. Removing the seeds from the top is called 'topping' the tobacco plants and is done with a sharp knife. The tobacco plant stem can be very hard, so cutting the tops off requires a good deal of strength. While Fred was in the tobacco field with a couple of other men cutting off these tops, he pulled the knife firmly and as it came through the plant stem it gashed into the wrist of his other hand. During this time in our lives, we were learning about the amazing healing miracles of Jesus and that these miracles were also ours to use under the authority of Jesus. Fred had actually been praying for God to show him a miracle if this was indeed biblical truth. Fred said that as soon as he felt the knife go into his wrist, he knew it was bad. Fred said that the cut was so deep that he could see those white ligaments halfway into his wrist. Fred said that as the two other men prepared to rush him to the hospital in hopes of saving his hand, Fred knew it was not God's plan. Fred dropped to his knees and asked God to heal the huge gash in his wrist. Fred recalls pulling his hand back toward his forearm and holding it tightly with the other hand, while asking God to "show" him great healing. I'm sure the other two men in the field that day expected Fred to bleed to death as he refused to leave the field and go to the hospital. Fred said that as soon as he asked God to heal him, there was no bleeding.

He said that the cut just seemed to 'stick' back together and he wrapped a rag around it to keep the area clean and went back to work. Fred arrived home that evening and told me about the event and that God had healed the huge gapping cut on his wrist. When I looked at his wrist, it had the appearance of a cut which had healed over several weeks. There was a definite raised healed ridge the entire width of his wrist where the cut had been and upon inspection it was incapable of being opened. It was totally healed closed. There was no redness on the wound site or around it, which you might expect from a wound caused by a dirty knife. The circulation to Fred's hand was great. Since the cut had obviously cut down through veins and arteries, you would expect no circulation into the hand. Now, God was fully capable of healing that wrist without any sign of a scar on the location, yet that scar formation proved it had occurred. Without that scar, no one would have believed it had happened in the first place, except for the two guys in the field with him, who saw the wound depth and the white ligaments. God had healed Fred's deep cut! What the enemy had planned as a tragic event was turned into a healing event for God's glory.

We had built our dream retirement home on the lake and had moved from the double wide trailer into our site-built home the spring of 2009. Not only had God provided this great building site for the construction of our home, he had his hand on every part of the construction process and God put together a team of Christians to build the house. It was delightful to enter the home under construction and hear Christian music filling the space. Everyone worked so well together and there was never a harsh word spoken. Every board and every nail placed in the house were put there by this Christian construction team and the result has been a peaceful retreat. I prayed over the house and the property lines for safety for the family and dedicated the property to God. The property is lakefront and the property elevation allows for the perfect view across the lake to the mountains in the distance.

There are times when things happen that God could have prevented, yet allowed to occur for his glory. Although the enemy may have had plans for a worse outcome, God reduced the outcome. This is the case for a most recent event, when my son David and daughter Jessica were enjoying riding their jet skis on the lake. David was riding alone on his jet ski while Jessica was riding as a passenger behind her husband, Matt, on their jet ski. They had been riding their jet skis for a short time that day when I received a phone call from Jessica's husband. He had called from his cell phone to say that there had been an accident and Jessica was hurt. They had been on the lake, close to the edge of our property when the accident occurred and his truck was down near the edge of the lake, so he was bringing Jessica up to me. He said that she was "having trouble breathing and that she could not feel her legs." The next few moments felt like an eternity as I waited and prayed for Jessica's arrival. As Fred and I waited for Jessica's arrival, I asked him if he remembered how to perform CPR. It sounded like her condition was critical and I would need help in the event CPR was required. Fred had such a look fear in his eyes as I said those words. I prayed healing for Jessica prior to her arrival and rebuked any plans the enemy had made that day. I proclaimed health and long life for Jessica without any physical limitations. When Jessica's husband arrived at the door with Jessica within 2 minutes, I could see the fear in his eyes, as he handed her off to my care. His eyes were saying, "Please fix her." As I laid Jessica on the couch her breathing was shallow and she was not making any sense in her attempts to speak. I immediately prayed healing over her body as I ran my hands all over her body. As I touched her body the Holy Spirit showed me where to touch to heal broken bones. I gently touched her left upper leg, her left ribs, her pelvis, and her left hip as I continued to pray for God to totally heal her in the name of Jesus. The Holy Spirit was telling me that she was healed and that there would be no broken bones or internal injuries. The Holy Spirit said there would be bruising and pain. As I placed some ice cubes into a zip-lock plastic bag and placed it on Jessica's left hip area, she looked up at me and said, "It really hurts there." Praise God! Yes... it did hurt and yes she was making sense. I don't think that she remembered me praying all over her body and touching the various areas as I prayed. Her breathing was regular now and she was able to take deep breaths.

Jessica's memory of the event is only that her brother's jet ski had run into her. David and Matt told the story of the accident and how the collision of the two jet skis occurred. They were both traveling at a high rate of speed and accidently turned toward each other too tightly. David's Jet Ski collided into the left side of Jessica's Jet Ski exactly where she was sitting and David's Jet Ski became airborne. The jet ski traveled up Jessica' left side and landed upright in the water on the other side of their jet ski. The entire weight of David's Jet Ski had been on Jessica as the Jet Ski went over top her and landed on the other side. It was amazing that Jessica was alive and I praised God for sparing her life.

As I prayed that night thanking God for his protection over my children that day, the Holy Spirit told me that it had been the enemy's plan to kill both my children that day. As these words from the Holy Spirit rested into my spirit, the Holy Spirit showed me that David's Jet Ski was supposed to flip upside down after it had gone airborne and drown him in the muddy edge of the lake. The plan of the enemy was that Matt would be so concerned with Jessica's injuries, that he wouldn't notice that David was under the water. God's protection that day saved both my children. Thank you Lord for your protection! To you be all the praise and Glory!

It would be days later when I could finally allow my self to look at the Jet Skis and see the total damage. The deep gouges on the under side of David's jet ski show the force of which it hit Jessica's Jet Ski as it was going over it. The deep gouges on Jessica's Jet Ski show the force of impact and the shredded seat on which she was sitting leaves me to know, that without God's protection that day, Jessica would not be with me today. As I was looking at the Jet Skis the Holy Spirit said, "When you prayed protection for your property you forgot the lake." Oh my GOD! I had forgotten to pray protection for my family while in the water and on the water. How could I have missed that? As I stood there in the back yard, I turned and faced the lake and declared safety for my family in and on that water. I declared safety for anyone leaving our property and entering into the lake either swimming or using any type of water craft and any type of lake toys. In the name of Jesus, I prayed protection over the lake.

After the accident Jessica did go to have x-rays taken to be sure there were no internal injuries or fractures. The doctor was amazed that there was nothing broken as a result of a

Jet Ski collision. The doctor took extra x-rays looking for hidden fractures, as he has never seen this type of collision without fractures. There were no internal injuries and no broken bones. Of course we knew that there had been yet God had totally healed Jessica that day with his mighty healing power. Praise God! To God be all the Glory... forever!

Psalm 32:7

"You are my hiding place; you will protect me from trouble and surround me with songs of deliverance."

Chapter 26

The truth will set you free!

✝

I had completed the previous chapter, which I thought would be the last chapter of this book and felt content that I had completed the task God had placed before me. Before going to bed, I asked the Lord to review the contents of this book and to let me know what else, if anything should be included. I fell off to sleep and slept soundly until 2:30 AM. I awoke suddenly at the Lord's prompting with words running through my mind. The book was not finished. The assignment was not complete until the offering of Jesus Christ as their personal savior was presented. Yes, the last chapter was to include the sinner's prayer to allow anyone who had not yet given their lives to Jesus, would know what to say in the privacy of their own home. Yes Lord, I will do that in the morning. Thank you Lord. As I rolled over to go back to sleep... there would be no sleep. The Holy Spirit was now heavy on my mind telling me to tell you about the great deceptions. Deceptions? Lord, what would you want me to tell them about deceptions? I am sitting up at my computer now as the Lord is flowing thoughts into my mind and onto this page. The vision that the Lord had given me and I had shared in a pervious chapter about seeing people pushed to the edge of a cliff and falling into the flames of hell in church pews, is again flashing through my mind. There is deception in the church that will prevent many from accepting Jesus as their personal savior. Many are not reading the Bible for themselves to know the truth about salvation. Many are depending on their pastor or priest to train them, and thereby lay the deception. There are false teachings being presented that will prevent you from accepting the Lord Jesus Christ as your personal savior. Lord, please show me these deceptions, so that I may share them with your people. There are so many deceptions flooding my mind right now, that I am amazed. It is now 3:00 AM and I am set forth on a task to reveal deceptions that have been given to his people through the church. I keep hearing over and over... there is one true God... Only your Heavenly Father can forgive your sins... no man on earth can do that... let no man deceive you... to receive your salvation through the blood of Jesus Christ, you must make that decision for your-self...no one can make that decision for you...

no prayer by someone else can save you... It cannot be done on your behalf when you are an infant... taking of the communion wine and bread is in remembrance of Jesus' sacrifice and does not save you... wow Lord! Are people actually being taught these deceptions in church today? Lord, show me. I need to see where each falsehood is taught, so I can warn your people. I have said Yes Lord, now show me. The Lord was gentle to say "use your computer and Google each religion with the word deception and the truth will unfold." Wow Lord, you use the computer? Now I'm laughing out loud, hoping not to awaken my husband at this hour. Of course, God can use the computer!

What I found when I Google searched a <u>specific religion/ deception.</u>
<u>Scientology/deception</u>
Web site: <u>www.cs.cmu.edu</u>

- Believe in reincarnation
- Christ has no essential or central place in the teaching
- No salvation principles.

Jehovah's Witness/ deception

Web site: www.christiananswers.net

- Teach that before his earthly life Jesus was a spirit creature, Michael, the archangel.
- Jesus is a God but not The God.

Catholic/ deception

Web site: www.evangelicaloutreach.org/ rcdeception.htm

- Taught they are all born again at infant baptism.
- They receive Christ when they partake of the communion wafer.

- Think that wearing the 'brown scapular' at their time of death assures that they will not suffer the fires of hell.
- Confess their sins to a priest instead of God.
- Hoping to enter Purgatory and there get purged of their sins to afterward get to heaven.

There are many more religions. These are the three that God placed on my heart to complete for you. I am not a religion scholar, so I am totally reliant on the content of the web sites I listed above. I encourage you to complete a Google search by listing <u>your religion/ deception</u> in the search bar and research what deceptions there may be in your specific religion. See what lines up with the Bible and what does not line up to the truth. If your church has deceptions that are not biblical truths, then leave that church and find a true Bible-believing church. Please don't go to a church just because your parents and grandparents did. Just because you were 'born into' a situation does not mean that you can not grow and thirst for God's truth.

The truth will set you free. Read what the Bible has to say. Some verses that the Holy Spirit gave me to include in this book are:

John 3;16, John 14:3, John 14: 6-7, Galatians 2:2, 1 Peter 2: 24, 2 Peter 2: 1-22, 1 Timothy 4: 1-2
2 Timothy 4: 3-4, 1 John 1:9

Don't look back

God has given me this word repeatedly and I feel it is important to include in this last chapter. The Bible tells us that no man who has set his hands to the plow and looks back is fit for the kingdom of heaven (Luke 9:62). In the day of Sodom and Gomorrah, when Lot and his wife were told to leave the city and not to look back, yet his wife did look back and became a pillar of salt (Genesis 19:26). Lot's wife looked back and it cost her life. When Peter was walking on the water, when he took his eyes off Jesus he started to sink. He was proceeding forward in faith walking on the water yet when he lost his focus on Jesus and looked at his circumstances; he started to sink into the water quickly (Matthew 14: 29-31). I must tell you... when Jesus returns to take you up to meet him in the sky... do NOT look back. Keep your eyes on Jesus and move forward to claim your reward. Look only forward at Jesus. As soon as you see Him do not take your eyes off of Him. This can not be the time to look upon your friends or family, or to look back at the earthly belongings that you are leaving behind. Should you look back to what you are leaving behind or to who you are leaving behind, you may well be left behind to suffer the tribulation. Keep your eyes upon Jesus. This is a one-man journey as you meet Jesus. You cannot take anyone with you that had not received Jesus as their personal savior. Each person must make this journey alone. I will say this again... Do not look back. Looking back will not help them, but will harm you. Keep your eyes on Jesus. Don't look back. Keep your eyes only on Jesus. The Holy Spirit really wants this repeated. DO NOT LOOK BACK. KEEP YOUR EYES ON JESUS. Jesus is coming soon.

The sinner's prayer

To accept Jesus as your personal savior you must make the decision for yourself and you must ask Jesus yourself. No one can do this for you. You must acknowledge that you are a sinner and that Jesus is the son of God who died on the cross for your sins in your place. You must ask God to forgive your sins and to wash you white as snow by the blood of Jesus. Ask him to come into your heart and direct your life. There are many variations of the prayer yet essentially including the items above is all that is needed. You can say additional things such as telling him how much you love him or listing out your greatest sins. It is not necessary to list out all your sins since asking him to forgive them all, covers them all. Listing them out loud will impede the enemy from reminding you later of those sins and that you didn't ask forgiveness for them. You can laugh in his face and tell him that Jesus has forgiven them.

I have heard many wealthy people say that they could never accept Jesus as their Savior since they would need to give up everything they own to follow Jesus. The verses in the Bible Matthew 19:24, Mark 10:23 and Luke 18:25 have been so widely misunderstood that many have thought it was purely 'impossible' to have money and enter Heaven. The thought of a 'camel fitting through the eye of a needle' is physically impossible, so why even consider that as an option. I remember thinking that as well, since after all... nothing can fit through the eye of a sewing needle... right? On a trip to the Holy land in 1998, my eyes were opened when the tour guide answered this question very clearly. When the Bible was translated into our English language, the words "eye of the needle' were used as the closest form of translation, yet not a completely accurate translation, as the Hebrew language has more words for each topic. The Hebrew words are so much more specific then our generic English language. As we use adverbs and adjectives to enhance our language, their Hebrew language includes the additional description in the actual word. A great example would be that in Hebrew there are numerous words to mean *love* and in the English language we only have *one* word for love. In Israel, the eye of the needle is an area of a path or wall of a very tight fit that would require the load to be removed from the camel in order to fit through the narrow space. Since with side walls on both sides are made of rock, the camel could not be forced to fit through the small area unless the entire load was removed to make the pass. Therefore it is not *impossible* for the camel to pass through the tight place; it is only required to pass through the narrow area alone. When I think about this, I think about the old saying…"You can't take it with you." So, it is not impossible for someone with great wealth to enter the kingdom of heaven… they will only be required to remove their stuff first. God may

Use Me, Lord

require them to give money to the poor or to support a ministry. I believe that God blesses his people so that others can be blessed. It is a lie of the enemy that Christians should not have money. God wants to prosper his people! The enemy has kept many Christians poor, by believing this lie about money. As long as you do not make money your idol there is no sin in your wealth. When anything, including money, becomes your main pursuit of life, then Jesus is not your first love. It's not money that's evil. It's anything that you put first in your life before Jesus. Go ahead... get rich... with integrity and by honest means of course, so you can bless others and please God. Go ahead...Accept Jesus Christ as your personal savior! You have nothing to lose and everything to gain.

The <u>only</u> way to the Heavenly Father is through His son Jesus Christ. If you have never said this prayer or can not remember having said this sinner's prayer, this is your day. When the Holy Spirit draws you to salvation you can feel it. There may be a racing of your heart or you may have become warm all over... or maybe, you can hear that still small voice saying... 'Say it my child'... Be obedient to His drawing. We never know when it may be too late. Our days are numbered and this may be your last day on earth. If you have said this in the past and have been away from God, just say it again. It's just like saying your wedding vows again after being married for 30 years. You are still married yet you want to say the vows again, because you love him so much. Go ahead... say them again. Just know that Jesus is watching you right now...make Him smile!

Dear Heavenly Father, I know that I am a sinner and have fallen short of the glory of God. I do not deserve to spend eternity

in Heaven with you. I know that your son Jesus died on the Cross for all my sins. I know that He died and rose again and sits at Your right hand interceding for me. I ask you to forgive my sins and wash me white as snow by the blood of your son Jesus Christ. Please come into my heart and direct my life. I love You and want to live for You. I want to spend eternity with You in Heaven. Thank you Lord. In Jesus precious name, Amen.

Sign your name right here if you said this prayer:

_____

*I*t doesn't matter if you plan to loan this book to someone else, it's great that they see you have made this decision. The next person who reads your book may need that encouragement. The best thing your book could have is multiple signatures under that prayer, indicating the book has been passed around and many have made the decision to accept Jesus as their personal savior.

If you said this prayer:

1. Write this date down. This date is more important than your birthday or you wedding day.

2. Tell someone! This is not something that you can keep secret. The Bible says that if we deny Jesus before men, Jesus will deny us before his father. If you have truly received Jesus as your personal savior, then tell someone.

3. Get baptized. Getting baptized is an outward act of obedience to show your inward decision to follow Christ. It symbolizes your new birth as you go beneath the water and then rise above the water.

4. Read your Bible. If you don't have one, buy one. Ask someone for one. Christians would be glad to give you a Bible. You must have your own Bible so that you

can read God's word for yourself. Never depend on someone else to teach you God's word.

5. If you have a version of the Bible that you don't understand, such as the King James Version, then go get one you can read and understand! I had a Kings James Bible for years and never could understand what God was saying until I got a NIV (New International Version). The NIV is written in our everyday language. There are no 'thee' and 'thou' in the NIV version. For the first time I was able to read and the Bible came alive to me. Religion says that we must have the King James Version. WHY? The kings James version is not the original text! The Bible was translated many years ago from the Hebrew, Aramaic and Greek. I understand that the new 'American Standard

Bible' has been 'literally word-by-word' translated from the original Bible text in recent years by Bible scholars and translators, and would therefore be a very accurate version and greatly improved over the King James Version. The version you chose is not as important as your ability to understand it.

6. Get into a church that teaches the Bible. Research on-line or ask a Christian friend, to find a church that believes Jesus is the son of God and believes the entire Bible. Don't get involved in a church that uses another 'book' other then the Bible. Fellowshipping with other believers will strengthen your Christian walk and give you true friends to face tough times with.

7. I would love to hear from you, although… I am not keeping any lists. God has written your name in the Book of life. He

has the list. I will see you in Heaven my brother or sister in Christ. Please enter my web site at www.incrediblemiracles. com and leave a testimony indicating that you made your decision to accept Jesus as your personal savior. Your testimony would be an encouragement to others who may be seeking the truth.

8. If I had some small part in your decision to receive Jesus as your Personal Savior, then Praise God! To God be all the Glory, forever and ever…

See you on the other side,

Helena

Website Changed to:
www.
incrediblemiraclesministries.
com

✝

A Special Thank You

First and foremost, I thank my Heavenly Father, Jesus and the Holy Spirit. Without them, this book would never have been written. To Them be All the Glory.

A special Thank You to my husband and best friend Fred, for his understanding and patience during the process of writing this book, and his own personal relationship with the Holy Spirit, knowing the outcome will far outweigh his time without me.

A special Thank you to my Children Jessica and David for allowing me to include their names in this book. Realizing that their lives will be affected by the contents of this book being revealed, they are confident in their relationship with Jesus, to allow this transparency to draw others to knowing Jesus Christ as their personal savior, whatever the cost.

A special Thank you to my daughter-in-law Tiffany and my son-in-law Matt for reading my manuscript prior to it's final proofing, to encourage me that the contents of this book are meant for this generation. I love you both dearly and thank our Heavenly Father for guiding you into our family.

Thank you to my friend Jean Ann Irwin for taking the time in her busy schedule to proof this book prior to submission to the publisher. Jean Ann is a busy professor at a local College, yet spent many hours in per personal time assisting with this project. Thank you Jean Ann!

May God pour more blessings on you then your wildest dreams could ever imagine!

Thank you to my friend Debbie Loyd, who has mentored me in the Lord for many years. Debbie has been patient with me and prayed without ceasing for my personal spiritual growth. Debbie has the sweetest spirit and I am proud to have her as a friend.

An 'Amazing' thank you to my granddaughter 'Aleisha Christina Marie' for her pure heart and amazing insight at her young age. She is only 2 ½ years old when this book is written and it will be several years before she is able to realize and understand the impact she had upon me while I was writing this book. Her words of knowledge given to me directly from 'Jesus' revealed the urgency of getting this book into the hands of this generation.

I know that I will forget someone in this process, so please forgive me, if you were left out. Our Heavenly Father knows what you have done and you will ultimately be blessed for your part.

LaVergne, TN USA
04 December 2010
207387LV00002B/2/P